EATING IN

FROM THE FIELD TO THE KITCHEN
IN BIOSPHERE 2

EATING IN

FROM THE FIELD TO THE KITCHEN
IN BIOSPHERE 2

BY SALLY SILVERSTONE

THE BIOSPHERE PRESS™

For my mother

THE BIOSPHERE PRESS™
A Division of Space Biospheres Ventures
Biosphere Road • Post Office Box 689 • Oracle, AZ 85623

THE BIOSPHERE PRESS and its logo are registered trademarks of Space Biospheres Ventures.

Food Editor: Molly Augustine
Editor and Art Director: Linnea Gentry
Recipe Editor: Lynn Ratener
Food Photography: Gill C. Kenny
Food Styling: Mary Seger
Production Coordinator: Kathy Horton
Designer: Kimura-Bingham Design
Cover Design: Debra Kay Niwa
Fruit photo on Title Page: John Cancalosi
Garden photo on Contents: C. Allan Morgan
Plate detail on Contents: Don Winston
Sunset photo on Contents: © Peter Menzel

Library of Congress Catalog Card Number 93-71192
Library of Congress Cataloging-in-Publication Data available upon request.

Manufactured in the United States of America
Printed by Arizona Lithographers

First Edition

ISBN 1-882428-04-8

Printed with soy-based inks on recycled and recyclable paper.

TABLE OF CONTENTS

Chapter **One**

TABLE FOR EIGHT

It's good food and not fine words that keeps me alive.

Molière

FOR AS LONG AS THE HUMAN RACE HAS BEEN MOUNTING EXPEDITIONS INTO THE UNKNOWN, WHETHER IT BE EXPEDITIONS TO CROSS OCEANS, TO REACH THE NORTH POLE, OR TO LAND ON THE MOON, FEEDING THE CREWS HAS BEEN A MAJOR PROBLEM. The details have varied greatly over time, ranging from how to preserve foods on long voyages before the days of refrigeration, to how to get food from container to mouth in conditions of zero gravity. As both the co-captain of our 'expedition' into Biosphere 2 and as the manager of the food systems, I was very much aware that the biospherian 'army' was going to be marching largely on its stomach and I had to ensure that that stomach was filled with an adequate, tasty diet. But no expedition in history has had to contend with as many or as complex problems in feeding its crew as ours has. And the reasons for this lie in the very nature of Biosphere 2 itself.

The first Biosphere 2 crew and their first anniversary feast.

Biosphere 2 was built as an apparatus with which to study our planet. By operating this apparatus and coming to understand the different processes that go on inside, we hope to come to a clearer understanding of how to better manage and preserve Biosphere 1 (the planet Earth). But unlike many research experiments, we must have a human crew inside the apparatus to monitor, manage, and conduct the research effectively. In the case of an essentially completely sealed, air-locked apparatus, such as ours, all the food must come from inside.

Growing enough food to feed the eight biospherians on a little over half an acre was certainly one of the greatest challenges we faced. The half acre included an area for field agriculture, a tropical orchard, and an animal area. The system had to be sustainable, which meant that it had to continuously recycle all its nutrients. It also had to be free of pollutants, which meant we could not use any chemical pesticides. The task of growing the food was particularly challenging during the first two-year mission, as Arizona received a record amount of rainfall and cloudy weather during both years. This meant that we had to deal with low yields due to low sunlight in addition to our pest problems.

The Intensive Agriculture Biome (what we came to call the IAB) was some eight years in the planning and construction. We investigated a large variety of agricultural systems during that time, including some that used not soils, but nutrient solutions fed to the plant roots, as well as the soil-based systems. A lot of the early work, particularly on cultivated domestic crops, took place at the Environmental Research Laboratory, a branch of the University of Arizona in Tucson, as well as in our own research greenhouses (an area called the Biospheric Research and Development Center, or the BRDC). Eventually we decided that, for ease of nutrient recycling and best yields, we would need a soil-based system in conjunction with a system to compost and recycle our waste and waste water back into the fields. As far as the cultivars were concerned, we were looking for the plants that would be the most successful in our combination of tropical environment and greenhouse-type conditions. Of course, this is an on-going process as we research and select more and more new cultivars. By the time we planted the IAB fields for the first time, we felt confident about our plan for the first mission. We had put together a system combining the old with the new. For example, we had incorporated an ancient Chinese method of raising fish, rice, and a water fern all together along with our computer-driven system for controlling temperature and humidity. Similar integrations of tradition and technology assist our survival throughout the Biosphere.

By the time the doors closed on September 26, 1991, our farm system was in full operation and all the biopsherians were fulfilling their respective

Overview of the Intensive Agriculture Biome.

roles in that system. Of course, we all joined together to harvest a plot or replant it, but we also had our own special areas of responsibility and interest. In addition to being manager of the field agriculture, Jane Poynter was the manager of the animal systems and took loving care of our goats. Mark Nelson was king of the basement, so to speak, which included the area we called the 'promenade duct'. This was an area open to sunlight at the south end of the basement housing planters, rice tanks, and our waste-water clean-up system, a complex arrangement of water, plants, and troughs to treat human waste. Mark operated this system and also took care of the plants down there. He was absolutely determined to use every ray of sun that fell into his area. Every time I thought we could not possibly cram in another pot or planter, he found another available spot. Linda Leigh and Roy Walford took special interest in the beans. Although our lab lab beans did well, Linda and Roy were eager to find additional, better-tasting types that would survive in our system. Linda tended the lab lab bean plots in the field area, and Roy ran bean experiments on the balcony running across the face of our apartments above the fields. Mark Van Thillo, known by everyone as Laser, took care of the compost and the worm-rearing boxes (the worms were fed to the chickens), and Abigail Alling, known as Gaie, tended the tropical orchard area. I had special charge of the vegetable patch as well as overall responsibility for the entire system from the planning, planting, and storing to cooking in the kitchen.

Even though we thought we were well prepared for the task, it did take some time to come to terms with the reality of our situation. We now had to produce everything ourselves from scratch. No more neatly butchered cuts of meat from the supermarket, no more packets or cans, no more reaching inside the cupboard for a plethora of herbs and spices, and, above all, no more sugar bowl or luscious slabs of butter or margarine. We did have approximatly three months' worth of food in storage when we closed the door. This was the food we had raised in the IAB prior to the closure. But otherwise, if we could not grow it ourselves, we could not eat it! Our black pepper plants, for example, did not produce flowers at all during the first experiment, so black pepper was off the menu from day one.

For all of us, these restrictions meant an adaptation to a completely new way of cooking. Some of the early attempts were awful. Our coarse, home-ground, whole-grain flours did not behave in the same way as store-bought flour; our meat was tougher than the cuts from the supermarket; and few of us had experience with our staple, the sweet potato, except to bake them for Thanksgiving Dinner once a year. Slowly a Biosphere 2 cuisine emerged as we each learned to experiment with the available food and find more creative ways of cooking. It wasn't always easy, but by the end of six months our sugar cravings had finally diminished, and we were appreciating the sweetness of fresh fruits. We had all grown out of the habit of throwing something into the hot oil of the frying pan and cooking it up for dinner, so we unanimously agreed it was better to eat our peanuts as a break-time snack rather than press them for oil.

Gradually the crew began to take great pride in inventing a new dish or a new use for a particular ingredient. I first started to record the recipes that we used as a legacy for future biospherian crews. However, it soon became apparent from the work of our resident medical officer, Roy Walford, that we were enjoying an exceptionally healthy diet. Our cholesterol levels dropped dramatically, and we all rapidly lost the excess weight that we had brought in with us. Both changes were due to the high-fiber, nutrient-dense, low-calorie, low-fat, sugar-free diet. It was also free of food additives and pesticides. As people on the outside began to show great interest in what we were eating and how we were preparing it, I realized that our experience and our recipes were worth sharing with more people than just the future crews and the outside staff.

So I began to hound the other biospherians to take note of the quantities they used when cooking. This was sometimes a problem, as the most inventive cooks would often just throw things into the pot, see how it tasted, throw in something else, and when they were done they would be unable to say how they got there. Soon creating a 'cookbook worthy' recipe became another matter of pride and the crew began to record their efforts.

I did not have time to test and double check all the recipes, so I enlisted help from the outside. Molly Augustine, who runs a conference center, complete with an organic garden, in France, and Lynn Ratener, on the Space Biospheres Ventures staff, started to test the recipes for me in their own kitchens. It soon became clear that there were one or two problems yet to be solved: several irate messages pointed out that fresh papaya, green bananas, fresh goat's milk, and some of Biosphere 2's other staple ingredients were just not readily available either in Tucson or in most of the rest of the United States. I began to include suitable substitutes that could be easily found in supermarkets but did not stray too far from the original Biosphere 2 recipe. Although my fellow crew members had for the most part lost their 'sweet tooths' and become accustomed to much more basic fare, my colleagues in Biosphere 1 had not, so I included honey as a possible option for those who like things sweet. Molly helped me take this a step further. She is adept at catering to very particular palates at the Les Marronniers conference center in Aix-en-Provence. So Molly added her magic touch to some of the recipes to make them even more appealing to others, as did Lynn.

Sally Silverstone weighing in the harvest.

In putting this book together, I felt I had to include more than just food items and recipes. The entire food process was a very big part of our story and I wanted to share some of the triumphs and disasters we experienced as we learned to grow our own, harvest our own, process our own, and cook our own. I hope our story will interest anyone who shares our enthusiasm for whole-food cooking, organic gardening, self-sufficiency, and a healthy diet. I have included caloric values, protein values, and fat values for those who are watching their weight. Even the desserts are, on the whole, low in fat and free of sugar and eggs and therefore of interest to those trying to avoid those foods. When using this book in your own kitchen, don't be afraid to invent for yourself. We came up with many different variations to the recipes included, often depending on what was available and in season. Have fun and happy eating! ❧

Chapter Two

OUT IN THE FIELDS

Maybe a person's time would be as well spent
raising food as raising money to buy food.

Fred A. Clark

By THE TIME THE DOORS OF BIOSPHERE 2 WERE SHUT ON SEPTEMBER 26, 1991, OUR HALF-ACRE FARM HAD ALREADY BEEN IN PRODUCTION FOR OVER A YEAR. Our Intensive Agriculture Biome (the IAB) consisted of the field crop area, the potagerie (a vegetable garden), the tropical orchard, and the animal barn. In the basement below the field crops we had collected the processing machinery that would transform our harvest into edible food. The kitchen and food processing room in the Habitat Area were completed in the last few weeks before closure. I was still unpacking equipment weeks after we shut the doors.

After a long process of selection and experimentation in the research greenhouses, we had ended up with the basic staples of beans, rice, wheat, sorghum, sweet potatoes, white potatoes, and peanuts. All of these crops took four months to mature inside the Biosphere, some of them longer in the winter months (due to the unusual cloudiness those first two years). As time passed, we learned more about the special needs of each crop. For example,

Wheat, sorghum, and rice were necessary staples.

SALLY SILVERSTONE

the sweet potatoes produced larger tubers if we kept them well pruned; the wheat would not produce as many seed heads if the temperatures were too high.

There were eighteen fields in all, and each field was approximately 1,000 square feet. In addition to the fields, there were other small growing areas like the planting boxes over the air vents, in the basement, and on the balcony. On the north side we had a grove of banana trees, and to the west we placed our rice paddies right near the windows so the rice could get all available sunlight. We tried to rotate our crops as far apart as possible, so that the same crops didn't grow in the same area twice in a row or side by side. This helped avoid build ups of disease or pests associated with certain crops.

At first it seemed to take us a long time to plant and harvest each one, perhaps because the harvest would often be in several stages, such as the sorghum. First we would cut the seed heads and store them in the oven to dry, then pull up the stalks and leaves for animal fodder and take the roots to the compost machine. The peanut fields seemed to take the longest, because they had to be completely uprooted to remove all the peanuts. Then all the nuts were picked from the roots and dried in the oven. We dried the greens to use as winter fodder, a great favorite with the goats. The peanut harvests were a great favorite with the humans, too. We all sat on upturned buckets, plucked peanuts, and made our estimates as to the bounty of the crop. The peanut crop was one of our main sources of fat, so it was very important to us.

Crop diseases and pests were no more a stranger to us in Biosphere 2 than they are to any other farmers. Our biggest problem, the broad mite, is not usually a major pest, but we had created the perfect conditions for it in the Biosphere. With practically no margin for error in such a tight space, the damage to our crops was really a serious problem. The mites would carry their young into the new leaf buds of the plants where they sucked nutrients from the plants and injected a toxin that made the leaves curl. So our new growth would be badly damaged. At one time we even tried to blast the mites with hot air from a hair dryer to get rid of them. Of course, since pesticides could not be a part of our small closed system, we could not fight them with chemicals. We were determined to get rid of them using biologically safe means. Pest control remains one area of research of great importance.

The field crops provided our staples, but it was the vegetables and herbs that brought the much-appreciated diversity to the diet. As manager of the potagerie, I soon learned what did and did not work. Mites destroyed my green beans crop after crop. Summer squash, however, did well year round providing I could stave off the powdery mildew. Cabbage and carrots did well in winter; bell peppers, eggplant, and chili produced all year.

The bananas are the Grand Nain variety.

ABIGAIL ALLING

Every morning I gathered vegetables fresh from the garden and brought them to the kitchen for the cooks. The herbs were scattered in various places. Mark raised some at the south end of the basement where the sunlight enters through ground-level windows and some on the balcony of the habitat. I had also planted herbs among the vegetables. Every day Mark brought a basket of fresh herbs to the kitchen.

Sweetness in our diet came from bananas, papayas, and other fruits planted along the north wall of the IAB and in the orchard. The banana was really the 'old reliable' of the food system. With comparatively little care and maintenance it produced in abundance, often helping us out when other supplies were low. We had to keep the new 'pups' pruned back to three or four per plant and occasionally prune off old leaves for fodder or prop up a plant loaded with a heavy bunch of ripening bananas. With this minimal attention, they continued to produce year round. Future crews will be able to enjoy mangos and avocados, but we got no fruit from our trees the first two years. Mushrooms were another delicacy that we hoped to raise, but all attempts to grow them failed — probably because we did not have a setup to maintain the correct humidity. So that's another challenge for future crews.

We had no refined sugars. Due to low levels of sunlight, the fruit trees

did not produce as abun-
dantly as we had hoped,
but we did get some occa-
sional figs, guavas, and cit-
rus. Banana and papaya
were probably the two
most useful crops in the
cooking as well as being
good producers. Banana
was a wonderful sweetener,

Banana trees line the back wall of the IAB.

and when reduced to a pulp it made a good thickener in many of our dishes. Cooked green it made a filling starch dish. We used ripe papaya in desserts, juices, and salads. As a green vegetable, it also made a wonderful thickener for soups or a filler for vegetable dishes.

Growing the food and harvesting it was only part of the work. After that it had to be rough processed and, in some cases, fine processed before it was in edible form. For example, after harvest we took the rice down to our huge drying ovens in the basement. After drying, we passed the heads through our threshing machine. The threshed grain would be caught in a tray beneath the machine for collection. We kept the straw for animal bedding on drying shelves in the basement. Other crop residues, such as stalks, leaves, and seeds, became animal feed. There was something about the basement that reminded me of legends of underground mines where strange creatures worked away never seeing the light of day — probably because it was always so dimly lit compared to the brighter sunlight upstairs. It was also quite noisy due to the air-handling machines (which kept our atmosphere circulating). This was the kingdom of the technosphere —

Threshing rice in the basement of the IAB.

pipes, cables, tanks, valves, wires, fuse boxes, and computers.

Strange as it was, I always felt quite happy in the basement, threshing away with the threshing machine. I think it was because I loved to get the final product of fresh, clean grain and weigh it in, even though it certainly took a significant amount of time. It had been hard to find machinery appropriate to our needs; we needed more than the hobbyist's type of 'do-it-yourself a time or two' home equipment and yet we could neither accommodate nor operate large, industrial processing machinery. The pieces we had settled on were somewhere between the two extremes, and some of it was rather small. Also, there was always safety to keep in mind. I was very aware of this, especially so after Jane suffered an accident soon after entering the Biosphere. While using the threshing machine, she had cut off part of her finger. Happily it healed well and quickly, but she now has a constant reminder of just how dangerous farm machinery is.

Some of the machinery, particularly the flour grinder, was very noisy. Part of this drawback was in the need to have all crew members always in touch by radio. If I was grinding flour, I always had to inform someone that I would be wearing my earmuffs for a while and could not hear the radio. So if anyone needed me, they just had to come get me.

Beans could have their hulls removed without the machinery. I discovered that the best procedure was to put them in a sack after they had been dried and then hit them for about five minutes with a rubber mallet. After that they could easily be put through the winnowing machine which separated the broken hulls from the beans. It was a very therapeutic activity; one could visualize that the sack was one's worst enemy and hammer away. I always recommended it to anyone who was feeling angry or aggressive.

The procedures that we used in the first mission really were the 'first shot', so to speak, at creating a totally self-sustaining, non-polluting agricultural system for Biosphere 2. As one would expect in any experiment, some things worked well and others did not. The things we learned in the first two years will be invaluable to us in continuing to develop not only this system but systems for future biospheres. ❧

Chapter Three

INTO THE KITCHEN

Man is a cooking animal. The beasts have memory, judgement, and
all faculties and passions of our mind . . . but no beast is a cook.
James Boswell

WHEN WE DESIGNED THE KITCHEN OF
BIOSPHERE 2 WE WANTED IT TO HAVE EVERY MOD-
ERN, TIME-SAVING CONVENIENCE POSSIBLE. After
all, it was going to take enough time and energy just to grow all our own
food. So in the kitchen we wanted the full advantage of twentieth-century
technology.

Margret Augustine, the co-designer of the project, searched high and
low for a dream kitchen. One day about a year before closure, she phoned
me from the Dallas airport. She had just discovered a magazine showing the
ideal kitchen and was determined to get it for us. The kitchen was very
expensive, but the layout was perfect and the fittings were indeed beautiful.
A deal was soon struck with the German manufacturer, Allmilmö, to get the
kitchen at a reduced rate in exchange for publicity. A few weeks before
closure I posed for the company photographers in the gleaming white
kitchen with my jars of beans and baskets of fresh vegetables arranged in
bright colors all around me.

Fresh vegetables varied daily.

But ours had to be much more than the typical gleaming, modern, family kitchen. Industrial-quality refrigerators and freezers were added to both the kitchen and the processing room, a large second kitchen and storage area behind the main kitchen. We had a dishwasher, microwave, wok, frying pan, two ovens, stove tops, etc. — all state-of-the-art electric equipment. (State-of-the-art equipment can have its drawbacks, as we were to discover. But that story comes later.) One of the biggest challenges of the kitchen was finding equipment that would last. We decided to go for plastic crockery and get as much unbreakable equipment as possible. Even so, the biospherian propensity for breaking kitchen equipment was remarkable. Crock pots burned out and electric kettles mysteriously stopped working. Some cooks even attempted to assist the blender with metal spoons, with disastrous results. Spatulas snapped in two and non-stick surfaces never failed to peel off. Luckily, we took in a lot of spares. For the next crew we will use industrial-scale equipment all round. On the whole I think we did a pretty good job in bringing in everything we needed. A better knife sharpener and some more microwaveable dishes would have been a help, but these will have to be added for future crews.

The food-processing room soon became known as the back kitchen. This is where I made bread, cheese, yogurt, pickles, and wine, activities which were all great favorites of mine. I loved to see what I could create out of the ingredients available and how to get a new unexpected taste into the diet. I had a small oven, a hot plate, and a sink in there, and I would often hide away for the afternoon making a surprise birthday cake or special treat. I stored the dry food on shelves here for up to one month at a time, doling it out each week for the cooks. I also had a notice board here for the cook of the day, where I would note how much of each ingredient they could use each day.

(Of course this varied from time to time depending on what was available.)

Food storage was something I had thought a great deal about before coming into the Biosphere, as I knew that we could not afford to let anything spoil. I had seen many traditional ways of storing food in my travels. In India, yogurt was kept fresh by putting it into a small clay pot inside a larger clay pot which was kept constantly wet. The evaporating water kept the inside cool. The Indian farmers also had an unusual method for storing rice. After the harvest, the rice straw was twisted into long, thick ropes that were then made into huge, coiled baskets. The rice would be stored all year in these coiled baskets.

But fascinating as it may have been, our crew would not have time for basket-making in the Biosphere. I purchased a large supply of plastic buckets with lids that could be hammered on air-tight. These were our main storage containers for the dry foods, such as beans and grains. Fresh foods were

The kitchen was designed with all the modern conveniences.

ALLMILMO

usually stored frozen. I discovered early on that we were going to have bananas in gluts. Several bunches would ripen at once and have to be stored to ensure a continuous supply. So we froze the bananas in small chunks or else in a pureed form; and it was still good for making desserts, but not as good as the fresh item. Beets I froze whole after cooking them just enough to remove their skins. At first I tried to dry and store herbs, but in the end it seemed much more satisfying to just pick them fresh every day as they were needed. The goat cheese froze very well and I always kept a supply of it in the freezer for celebrations.

Out of the way in the back kitchen I had all my brewing gear. Brewer's yeast was one of the supplies that we brought in. I found the best basic ingredient was banana. I would dry this in the oven and then cook up the dried banana and leave it to ferment (as described in the banana wine recipe in Chapter 7). During the fermentation process I could not resist frequently tasting the brew just to see how it was getting on, and I have to say that we often drank brews well before a home-made wine connoisseur would consider them fit for drinking.

Our kitchen was a mixture of the best of the old and the best of the new. On a shelf above the modern electric oven I had a porcelain pestle and mortar, probably identical to the one used by my great grandmother. On the storage shelves in the back kitchen I had the modern, plastic, freezer containers stacked next to old-fashioned, large, glazed clay jars that I used to salt down vegetables for sauerkraut and for which I never managed to find a modern substitute. I think the kitchen in Biosphere 2 is one of the places I will come to miss the most. It was really a pleasure to cook in, and I always looked forward to my turn. It made a pleasant break from the rest of the week's routine and gave me a chance to experiment with ingredients and invent new dishes.

When we ate a particularly delicious meal, we would often reflect on how long it took to prepare from planting and growing, to harvesting and processing, to cooking. We figured that our favorite dish, biospherian pizza, took at least four months. This was the time it took for the wheat crop to mature, not to mention the time to thresh it and grind it. Then there were the tomatoes and peppers and onions to go on top and the goat cheese made from milk. (We needn't go into the time it took to grow the fodder to feed the goats to produce the milk, etc! The story could go on forever.) But there was something really satisfying about knowing exactly where all the food we ate came from. It also pleased us that the food was free of pesticides, preservatives, and artificial colorings and flavorings. I know that after this two-year period when I am back in Biosphere 1, I'll enjoy the luxury of helping myself to basic staples, such as flour and rice from the shelves of a food store, but I find it hard to imagine that the meals will ever taste as good as they did in Biosphere 2. ❧

From the field to the kitchen to the dinner table — no small task.

Chapter Four

ABUNDANCE DOESN'T COME EASY

Then a sentimental passion of a vegetable fashion must excite your languid spleen,
An attachment à la Plato for a bashful young potato,
or a not too French French bean!

W.S. Gilbert

We NORMALLY CONSUMED EIGHT POUNDS OF STARCH A DAY AMONG US IN THE FORM OF RICE, SWEET POTATOES, WHITE POTATOES, PLANTAINS, OR TARO. As we had very little oil we could not deep fry anything, so we became very inventive in making our starch dishes interesting and tasty. The vegetables that were available varied according to the time of year and how well we were doing in the battle against the pests and diseases that affected them. By far the greatest culinary challenge amongst the vegetables was the taro. This very hardy tuber grew well in nooks and crannies all over the IAB. It required very little attention apart from generous watering and did not seem to be affected by diseases or pests. At times when all our other starch sources were dwindling, it was a reliable alternative. There was just one problem. No one liked to eat it. When we first started to cook it, several of the biospherians complained of burning sensations in the mouth and throat. Others declared that no matter how hungry they were, they just could not stand the taste.

I sent out requests for assistance in several directions. I was even sent

Lima beans before and after hulling.

a taro recipe book over the fax machine. However, no matter how exotic our cooking, the unmistakable taste and burn of taro remained. Eventually John Druitt, an old colleague of mine from Puerto Rico, came up with the solution. Taro is eaten a lot in the rural districts of the island, so John asked his Puerto Rican buddies about it and discovered that it was very important to peel the taro well to remove the non-edible acids. The second necessity was to cook it for a long time. We found that these steps removed the burning sensation. We gradually got clever at mixing the resulting starchy substance with several other strong ingredients, such as blending it into a really tasty soup or bean dish, to help hide the distinctive taste.

The sweet potato was one of our staples. If uninfested it did very well. We pruned it back regularly to encourage it to produce more tubers. The second year it was hit by a devastating attack of broad mites. These microscopic little mites when magnified look somewhat like a yellow gum drop with legs, and they managed to do an incredible amount of damage for their

The taro (left) is cultivated extensively in the tropics. Mark Van Thillo (right) with sweet potatoes.

MARK NELSON

size. The growing points turned brown and shriveled, and there were hardly any tubers formed when we harvested the fields. I had heard that research into controlling mites with vegetable oils had been successful, so we imported some horticultural oil to experiment with. Regular spraying certainly helped to control the mites over the winter months. But then we ran into a new problem: large holes

Spraying with horticultural oil helped to control mite infestations.

MARK NELSON

began to appear in the leaves. I could never see the culprit during the day, so one night I went out with a flashlight and found that cockroaches were happily grazing on the fresh leaves. I had never seen this before, but it dawned on me that it was happening just after an oil spray. Evidently we were providing the cockroaches with just the kind of salad dressing they relished on their greens! We immediately began to search for a parasite that would attack cockroach eggs and help to keep the cockroach population down.

As far as vegetables were concerned, by far the most popular were the squashes. The summer squashes were very good stir-fried. We usually baked the winter squash and ate everything, skin included, unless it was very hard. The seeds made a great snack roasted on their own or mixed in with rice. The stuffed pumpkin recipe, on page 36, invented by Mark looked very appealing on the table whenever we had a feast. In the winter we often had more leafy green vegetables than anything else, which were not too popular. There was one biospherian who insisted on making almost inedible sauces and soups out of pureed green leaves and little else. Eventually the person, who shall remain unnamed, was told that if this continued he would end up wearing his dingy green delicacies. The cooking took a turn for the better after that.

Tomatoes were by far the most popular ingredient, but for several reasons they did not grow abundantly in the Biosphere. In the summer the temperature regimes were probably too warm at night for them to set fruit, and in the winter they just did not get enough light. As the food systems manager I had to portion them out carefully amongst the cooks so that everyone got their fair share to cook with. I always intended to can tomatoes in the season when they did well so that we could have some later, but we always managed to eat every available one.

The growing of beans in the Biosphere was a continuous saga — it could almost be classified as a tragedy! We had originally planned our diet around a large variety of dried beans but found that they did very poorly, mostly due to mite infestations or powdery mildew. Time and again we planted fields of beans and watched them flourish and flower, only to see the pests move in and put an end to them. Eventually we realized that the common pinto and kidney beans were not going to make it and that we had to rely on a much hardier class of bean. One type was called the hyacinth or lab lab bean. This was an extremely hardy perennial that produced beans from October to June. They were rather oily and not too tasty alone, but with plenty of seasoning they could be made into a variety of palatable dishes. The goats loved the oily hulls and the milk production always went slightly up when they ate them. During the first two years of the experiment we continued to grow trial plots in the research and development greenhouses to find really reliable beans. Eventually, we should have a whole collection of beans that are 'Biosphere hardy' as well as tasty.

Of all the crops that we grew I found rice to be the most fun. The rice seedlings were raised on flats in the nursery and then transplanted into the newly drained rice paddies. I enjoyed the mud squishing between my toes as I planted the little seedlings, and they always looked so beautiful when new in the field. Having lived in India,

Rice harvesting was the most fun.

ABIGAIL ALLING

I have vivid memories of line after line of village women with saris hitched up to their waists bent over double placing the seedlings in the ground with swift rhythmic movements, singing as they went. I tried to set the same pace myself when transplanting but never quite succeeded. We did get very fast, though. Each rice planting season, of which there were three a year, seemed to get easier. The rice paddies were right next to the windows of the farm area, so visitors could often see us engaged in this age-old task. One part of the procedure was to catch all the fish in the paddy after we drained it and move them to another tank until we refilled the paddies. The fish would flip about in the mud and splatter it everywhere (including all over us) as we raced about trying to net them. Great visitor entertainment! I often looked up after netting a fish and found myself receiving rounds of applause from the onlookers.

The wheat harvest was also a pleasurable affair. The ripe, golden heads always contrasted so dramatically with the bright greens of the other crops.

Linda gathers up the wheat harvest for processing.

We would harvest it in large sheaves and carry them down to the ovens for drying. Wheat was by far the most popular grain for cooking. Without it we could not have made leavened bread or the all-important birthday cakes. Sorghum, however, was at the bottom of the popularity chart. It was not as tasty as wheat and most of the biospherians had some degree of allergic reaction to the pollen. When it came to harvest time, most of us broke out in hives where the plant came into contact with our skin. We had to be sure to wear long sleeves on our arms and bandannas round our necks.

The amount of grains and starches we had to cook with varied with the seasons. When there were no potatoes, we had to use green bananas as an alternative. Potatoes and bananas were used in many ways that I had never thought of before, such as a thickener for savory sauces and desserts. Sometimes we even used the green bananas as a thickener for the morning porridge if grain was in short supply.

The recipes here are very basic. We used a great many variations depending on what ingredients were available and thus tended to do something different each time we made a dish. So, as we do, use these recipes as a guide, and experiment with whatever you have available. ❧

Wheat was by far the most popular grain for cooking.

MARK NELSON

BEACH BLANKET BEAN BURGERS

I made these for our first beach party. They are very tasty, especially with the onion-dill buns. If you want meat in your burgers you can replace some or all of the beans with finely chopped, cooked chicken, beef, or pork.

BUNS FOR THE BURGERS
8 BUNS

1 1/2 cups warm water　　*4 cups whole-wheat flour*

1 teaspoon dry yeast　　*1/2 cup finely chopped onion*

1 teaspoon salt　　*3 teaspoons dill seed*

Mix the dry yeast into 1/4 of a cup of the warm water and leave until foamy. Mix the flour, salt, onion, and dill seed in a large bowl. Add the yeast mixture and the rest of the warm water and form the mixture into a ball. Knead on a floured surface for 10 minutes and then let rise in a bowl covered by a damp cloth for 1 hour. The dough should double in size. Divide the dough into 8 pieces and form balls. Place the dough balls on a lightly greased baking sheet and let rise again in a warm place for 15 to 20 minutes. Bake in a 400-degree oven for 15 minutes or until golden brown on top. When cool, cut in half and insert the burgers. Each bun will contain:

Calories 186 ▌ Protein 7g ▌ Fat 1g ▌ Cholesterol 0

BEAN BURGERS
8 BURGERS

3 cups of cooked beans
(kidney or pinto beans
are good)

1 medium onion,
finely chopped

1 large potato, cooked

2 large tomatoes, chopped

2 teaspoons chopped thyme
(or 1 scant teaspoon dry)

2 teaspoons chopped sage
(or 1 scant teaspoon dry)

3/4 cup breadcrumbs or
whole-wheat flour

salt and pepper to taste

Mix all the ingredients thoroughly, either in a food processor or with a potato masher. The cooked beans should be mashed, not pureed, and the mixture should form into balls easily. If the mixture is too wet, add a little more breadcrumbs or flour. Form the mixture into eight burgers and place them on a lightly greased baking tray. Bake at 350 degrees for 45 minutes, turning them over after 30 minutes. Place the burgers inside the buns and top with fried onions, lettuce, tomato, pickles, or whatever your taste dictates. Each burger will contain:

Calories 352 ▮ Protein 20g ▮ Fat 1g ▮ Cholesterol 0

BEAN BALLS IN CHEESE & TOMATO SAUCE
SERVES 6

BEAN BALLS

3 cups cooked soy, kidney, or
garbanzo beans

1 medium potato, peeled and
cooked

3/4 cup finely chopped green
onion or chives

1 small onion, finely chopped

1 celery stalk, finely chopped

1 tablespoon each thyme,
rosemary, and marjoram
(or 1 teaspoon each of
dried spices)

2 large cloves garlic, crushed

2 tablespoons parsley, chopped

salt and pepper to taste

1/2 cup bread crumbs or
whole-wheat flour

Mash the potato and beans together with a potato masher. Add the onion, celery, and herbs and mix well. Form the mixture into 24 small balls. Roll each ball in the bread crumbs or flour and place on a lightly greased baking sheet. Bake at 350 degrees for 30 minutes. Serve on a bed of rice covered with CHEESE AND TOMATO SAUCE.

CHEESE AND TOMATO SAUCE
SERVES 6

6 large tomatoes, chopped

1 large onion, chopped

1/2 cup fresh basil, chopped

1 large potato, peeled
  and cooked

4 cups of whey
  (see cream cheese recipe)
  or 8 ounces of
  soft cream cheese

salt and pepper to taste

Place onion, tomato, and basil in a pot with enough water to just cover and simmer for 10 minutes. Put the contents of the pot in a blender with the cooked potato and blend to a smooth consistency. Return the mixture to the pot and simmer gently for 20 minutes or until thick. Just before serving, stir in the whey and heat gently. If you are using cream cheese, whip it in a blender with enough water (up to 3 cups) to make a thick but pourable consistency. Stir into the tomato mixture and reheat gently. Do not allow the sauce to boil once you have added the cream cheese or whey. Pour over BEAN BALLS and rice for a well-balanced, one-dish meal. Each serving without the rice will contain:

Calories 607 ▮ Protein 30g ▮ Fat 14g ▮ Cholesterol 41mg

SWEET POTATO CASSEROLE
SERVES 4

CASSEROLE

2 large sweet potatoes, cooked (You can peel them, but the skins are tasty. Just remove any blemished spots.)

1 small onion, finely chopped and sautéed

2 teaspoons fresh sage, chopped (or 1 scant teaspoon dried)

1 tablespoon fresh thyme, chopped (or 1 teaspoon dried)

1 cup milk or yogurt (low fat)

1 teaspoon salt

TOPPING

1 sliced tomato

2 ounces cream cheese

pinch of dry basil (or a few teaspoons of minced fresh basil)

Blend all the casserole ingredients together in a food processor and pour into a 2-quart casserole dish. Dot the top with the cream cheese, cover with the slices of tomato, and sprinkle on the basil. Bake in a 350-degree oven for about 20 minutes, or until the cheese starts to turn golden. Serve hot. Each serving will contain:

Calories 419 ▮ Protein 8g ▮ Fat 14g ▮ Cholesterol 19mg

STUFFED PUMPKIN

SERVES 8

1 medium pumpkin
(8 to 10 inches in
diameter; choose
an attractive specimen
with no skin blemishes)

2 medium onions,
finely chopped

2 cloves garlic

2 teaspoons fresh sage (or
1 teaspoon dried sage)

1/4 cup chopped parsley

4 large sweet green chilies or
2 bell peppers, chopped

4 teaspoons vegetable oil

2 tablespoons lemon juice

salt and pepper to taste

Cut the pumpkin in half, scoop out the seeds, and place it cut sides up on a baking sheet. Bake in a 350-degree oven until the flesh is tender (about 1 1/2 hours). Remove from the oven and scoop out the pumpkin leaving about 1/2 an inch of flesh around the edges to give the pumpkin shell some strength. Sauté the chopped onion, garlic, chilies, and herbs in the oil. When the onion is translucent, add the scooped out pumpkin flesh and continue to sauté until everything is coated in oil and lightly fried. Season the mixture with salt and pepper and stir in the lemon juice. Return the mixture to the pumpkin shells and heat through in the oven for at least ten minutes. Serve hot. This dish is great for a buffet since it looks so attractive, and it's fun to scoop the mixture straight out of the shells. Each serving will contain:

Calories 137 **❙** Protein 3g **❙** Fat 7g **❙** Cholesterol 0

BANANA BEAN STEW
SERVES 6

2 pounds green bananas or
   plantains (or about 3 pounds
   weighed with their skins)

1 cup kidney or pinto beans,
   cooked

1 chopped jalapeño chili
   (or 1 tablespoon canned
   jalapeños)

1 large onion, chopped

1 tablespoon pork fat or
   vegetable oil

3 large tomatoes, pureed
   (or a 14-ounce can of
   stewed or pureed tomatoes)

salt and pepper to taste

Peel the green bananas or plantains. The skin comes off easily by cooking them in the microwave until they turn black, about 10 minutes. Slice the bananas into 1/8-inch disks and cut each disk in quarters. If you don't have a microwave, peel the bananas, boil them for about 10 minutes until they begin to get soft, and then slice. Melt the pork fat (or heat the oil) in a large frying pan or wok and sauté the onion and chopped chili for a few minutes. Add the beans and banana slices, continuing to sauté until they are coated in oil. Pour the pureed tomatoes over the bananas and beans. Add enough water to cover the whole mixture and simmer for about 40 minutes or until the bananas are tender. Serve hot. Each serving will contain:

Calories   308   ▌ Protein   10g   ▌ Fat   6g   ▌ Cholesterol   0

ROY'S POTATO/TOMATO CAKES
8 LARGE CAKES

2 pounds white potatoes, cooked

1 onion, finely chopped and sautéed

1 teaspoon salt

1 tablespoon each fresh chopped marjoram, basil, and sage (or 1 teaspoon each of dried spices)

Mash the potatoes lightly until they are in small chunks, not a paste. Mix in the herbs and onion, and shape the mixture into a loaf. Slice the loaf into 8 pieces and place on a greased baking tray. Spread salsa on the potato cakes or top each with a thick tomato slice sprinkled with parsley. Bake in a 350-degree oven for 20 minutes. In the Biosphere these were always welcome for breakfast since they made a hearty way to start the day. They also make a fine lunch, served with a crisp green salad.

SALSA

6 medium tomatoes, chopped

2 tablespoons parsley, minced

1 large clove of garlic, minced

1 green pepper, finely chopped

1 hot jalapeño pepper, finely chopped

2 tablespoons oil

To make the salsa, sauté the green pepper, hot pepper, and garlic in the oil until tender. Add the tomato and herbs and let simmer for 20 minutes. If you top the cakes with salsa each cake will contain:

Calories 177 ❙ Protein 3g ❙ Fat 7g ❙ Cholesterol 0

Peanut Fried Rice
SERVES 4

1 ½ cups brown rice, cooked
    (white rice can also be used)

1 small onion,
    finely chopped

2 cloves garlic, chopped

2 tablespoons chopped
    green onion or chives

2 tablespoons oil

1 cup of roasted peanuts
    (Don't use the greasy,
    salted kind. Buy a bag of raw
    shelled peanuts and roast
    them on a baking tray in
    a 325-degree oven for
    20 minutes, turning
    frequently.)

salt and pepper to taste

This simple rice dish can be served hot or cold. In a large pan sauté the onion and garlic in the oil until tender. Add the peanuts and sauté for about five minutes. Add the cooked rice and green onion and toss all the ingredients in the pan until well mixed. Serve hot immediately, or chill and serve as a cold rice salad, either plain or tossed with a light vinaigrette dressing. Each serving will contain:

Calories 442 ▮ Protein 12g ▮ Fat 22g ▮ Cholesterol 0

Bird's Nests
SERVES 6

6 hard boiled eggs

1 raw egg

$1/8$ cup milk

see ingredients for
BEAN BALLS,
page 32

Shell the hard boiled eggs. Follow recipe for BEAN BALLS and form a 1-inch thick layer of the bean mixture around each egg, taking care to keep the egg in the middle. You should now have six large egg-shaped balls. Beat the remaining raw egg with the milk. Coat each ball in the egg-milk mixture and then toss each ball in the breadcrumbs or flour. Bake them on a lightly greased baking dish in a 350-degree oven for about 40 minutes, turning occasionally. Before serving, cut each ball in half exactly down the middle revealing the egg inside. This dish may also be served with CHEESE AND TOMATO SAUCE. Each serving (without the sauce) will contain:

Calories 512 ❚ Protein 33g ❚ Fat 8g ❚ Cholesterol 320mg

Stuffed Eggplant
SERVES 6

3 medium eggplants

2 tablespoons
chopped parsley

1 lemon for garnish

$1/2$ recipe of
HOT FISH SAUCE, page 75

Prepare HOT FISH SAUCE. Cut the eggplant in half lengthwise. Scoop out part of the flesh leaving 1/2 inch around the shell. Cut the flesh into small cubes and add to the fish sauce. Place the shells upright on a lightly oiled baking tray or casserole dish and fill them with the fish-eggplant mixture. Bake at 375 degrees for about 40 minutes or until the eggplant is tender. Garnish with chopped parsley and lemon slices. Each serving will contain:

Calories 201 ❚ Protein 17g ❚ Fat 53g ❚ Cholesterol 41g

WHOLE-WHEAT SOURDOUGH BREAD
TWO 9-INCH LOAVES

SOURDOUGH STARTER

2 cups whole-wheat flour   *1 tablespoon yeast*

2 cups warm water

Mix the ingredients together, cover the bowl, and leave it somewhere fairly warm for at least 6 days. Every time you make bread, use all the starter except 1 cup. Take this cup and add another cup of flour and 2 cups of warm water. This gives you the next starter. Again, next time you use it, reserve one cup and add one cup flour and 2 cups warm water, and so on. You can use the starter again the next day or leave it unused for 3 or 4 days. If you want to leave it longer than that, store it in the refrigerator and bring it out the day before you want to use it.

The night before, place the following ingredients in a bowl :

6 cups of whole-wheat flour   *All the sourdough starter*

2 teaspoons salt   *(except for one cup)*

Stir the mixture well and leave overnight in a warm place. The next morning, divide the dough into two bread tins and let it rise for 1 hour. The dough will not be like kneaded bread dough; it will resemble a very thick porridge. Bake the bread in a preheated oven at 400 degrees for 40 minutes.

To vary the bread, add any of the following:

1 cup finely chopped mixed fresh herbs

2 teaspoons of fennel seed or anise seed

1 cup finely chopped fresh chives or 2 crushed cloves of garlic

1 teaspoon dill seed or ground coriander

If you divide each loaf into eight slices, each slice will contain:

Calories 165 **|** Protein 7g **|** Fat 1g **|** Cholesterol 0

Chapter Five

THE POTAGERIE

Beautiful soup, so rich and green,
Waiting in a hot tureen!
Who for such dainties would not stoop!
Soup of the evening, beautiful soup!
Soup of the evening, beautiful soup!

Lewis Carroll

FRESH VEGETABLES STRAIGHT FROM THE GARDEN WERE PRIME INGREDIENTS IN OUR CUISINE. We had a salad at nearly every meal made from what we picked fresh that day. We often made a dressing using pureed banana which was delicious to us, but I would not recommend to others. As we had no oil, other types of dressings were a little difficult to make; the most popular one was the yogurt dill dressing. Fresh vegetables were also important ingredients in our soups. In fact, we relied heavily on the potagerie and the herb garden to provide color and variety to our entire diet.

A large bowl of soup, enough for at least two servings each, was always the main part of our lunch. We soon discovered that the quickest, easiest way to make a tasty soup was to cook it in the crock pot overnight. These slow cookers are easily found, and you don't have to continuously watch and stir them. All of the soup recipes in this chapter can be cooked either in the crock pot overnight or on the stove top. If you cook them on the stove top, plan to

Fresh herbs were important to all salads and soups.

ABIGAIL ALLING

simmer them gently for two to three hours to get a really good flavor. None of the recipes call for frying ingredients before cooking, and since potato is usually used as the thickener, these soups make a great low-calorie, low-fat meal. The stock was usually vegetable-based, but on the days after a meat meal we used stock made from meat bones for an especially rich soup. The whey left over from cheese making was also a delicious soup stock. It required a light, delicate touch and a good instinct with herbs to make a good soup. Linda was one of our best soup makers, and Jane's tomato soup was another all-time favorite. The only problem was that every soup was slightly different depending on what I had managed to bring up from the farm that day. I always had trouble getting the biospherians to remember how they had made their soup when one turned out to be especially tasty. For example, Linda once made a really delicious eggplant soup, but neither Molly nor I ever managed to replicate it exactly or get the recipe to a point where we could include it here. It must have been her own magic touch.

The potagerie was my responsibility, an obligation I undertook very willingly. I inherited my love of growing vegetables from my grandmother who tended her own garden in London. My earliest memories of visits with her involve picking and stringing beans and then packing them away in salt. We also picked berries from her raspberry vines to make into jam. Growing vegetables as a hobby is very different, however, from providing a major part of the daily food for eight people. I had one plot of land in the farm area devoted entirely to vegetables, which rotated yearly. It was divided into strips of seasonal vegetables. In the winter I concentrated on the cool weather crops such as carrots, cabbages, and greens. In the summer the garden would be full of summer squash and beans. When everything was thriving, it was my favorite place to be. The different greens of the lettuce, squash, and carrots contrasted beautifully with the red leaves of cabbages or the purples of rhubarb, chard, and beets to make a striking patchwork. Nothing was more pleasurable than going through with my bucket to collect the bounty. I also had the job of playing chief pollinator to the squash. Our bee population had dwindled greatly, much to our disappointment. Somehow they just had not adapted to the conditions of Biosphere 2, or maybe there was not enough food available for them in the early days of the experiment. We certainly have not given up on bees for pollination and will be introducing them again for the next mission. But for this mission I had to take over. I went from plant to plant sprinkling the pollen from the male flowers into the female flowers, eating the flower petals as I went.

When things were not thriving, I was in despair (a condition I am sure all gardeners, no matter how small a patch they have, will sympathize with). Every time I saw the white patches of powdery mildew appear on the squash, I feared that I was in for a losing battle. Yet we often battled with various pests and won. Aphids loved to eat the eggplants, but we found we could wash them off daily with a heavy water spray. Broad mites devastated the peppers, waiting until all the delicate, white, bell-like flowers were open to move in and turn the resulting fruits brown, deformed, and stunted. Fortunately, we found that regular spraying of horticultural oil and good pruning kept the mites at bay.

Both years we put at least one entire plot into beets over the winter. They always grew reliably even in low light levels and provided a high amount of calories. At first everyone was delighted to have them, but when we had a really bumper harvest the novelty began to pall. Beets appeared on the table at every meal in various forms and guises. Beet soup, mashed beet, beet and potato patties, boiled beets, beet juice, beet salad, beet dessert. We even tried to create a recipe for beet wine. We finally drew the line when someone tried to serve beet porridge for breakfast. And then the new name, the Beetospherians, was proposed. Taber, our resident pun artist, made so many puns about beets that at one stage we made threats against his person if just one more pun slipped out. The first year everyone heaved a sigh of relief when we ate the last bag of frozen beets. But by the time the second winter came around, they were once again a welcome sight on the dinner table as the produce from other plots diminished.

Another important ingredient in soups were the fresh herbs. We began by trying to grow herbs in the south end of the basement where the sun shines in through a long row of windows. But there was not enough light. Mark found that almost all his efforts to keep up a continuous supply of herbs came to naught. So we gradually transplanted all the herbs out of the basement. We ended up with herbs tucked into every nook and cranny in the IAB. They did particularly well on the balcony, so this is where we concen-

trated them. Fresh chives, basil, oregano, mint, thyme, and sage were
nearly always available. We grew dill
and fennel for the leaves and seeds. We
had cardamom plants in the orchard,
but they did not produce pods during
the first two years. We had some success with spices. Ginger has grown well
and we had a good crop of tumeric. I
think the spices I have missed the most
are cinnamon, nutmeg, and cloves.
Our cinnamon tree in the rainforest

A "Beeto-spherian."

was too small to harvest during the first two years, and we didn't find a
nutmeg or a clove tree to install before closure.

One thing we did have in continuous and plentiful supply year round
were chili peppers. We had several different types, including the large green
variety and little bright-red variety. They were so hot you had to be very
careful not to use too many. They all grew really well even in low light. At one
stage, the soups and stews got hotter and hotter as some of the crew members
competed to see who could eat the hottest food. Eventually I put my foot
down as food systems manager, since those of us who did not wish to compete
for this honor were having trouble stomaching the meals! The hot chili
enthusiasts, Roy and Taber, resigned themselves to making their own
chopped chili relish to sprinkle on their food. ❧

TOMATO SOUP HARLEQUIN
12 LARGE SERVINGS

This is a really simple tomato soup created by Jane. Dried herbs can be used instead of fresh, using half the quantity, but the fresh herbs really make this soup.

4 pounds of tomatoes, quartered

1/2 cup chopped fresh basil (or 3 tablespoons dried basil)

1/4 cup chopped fresh oregano (or 2 tablespoons dried oregano)

1 medium onion, chopped

2 potatoes, sweet or white

salt and pepper to taste

Garnish:

1/2 cup freshly chopped parsley

1 cup plain yogurt

Place all the ingredients in a 4-quart crock pot. Fill with water and cook overnight. At least 1 hour before serving blend all the ingredients together in a blender and return to the crock pot. Cook slowly for 1 more hour. Garnish with freshly chopped parsley and a spoonful of plain yogurt. Each serving with garnish will contain:

Calories 63 ▮ Protein 3g ▮ Fat 1g ▮ Cholesterol 1.2mg

BIOSPHERE BEET SOUP
SERVES 8

3 pounds beets

1 large potato

1 lemon, juiced

8 cups of beef or vegetable stock

salt and pepper to taste

yogurt for garnish

Cook the beets and potato in water to cover until soft. Then blend the beets and the potato until smooth using a little of the cooking water. Pour in a saucepan and add the vegetable or beef stock and the lemon juice. Simmer gently for half an hour, adding more water if the soup is too thick (although it should be very thick). Serve with a large dollop of yogurt in each bowl. Each serving with yogurt will contain:

Calories 101 ▌ Protein 4g ▌ Fat 0.25g ▌ Cholesterol 0.2mg

HEARTY PEA SOUP
SERVES 8

3 cups dried peas

1 cup chopped onion

6 medium carrots, chopped

2 large sticks of celery, chopped

1 tablespoon fresh thyme

(or $^1/_2$ teaspoon dry)

A soup bone for flavoring, either beef or pork (optional)

3 cups milk (optional)

salt and pepper to taste

yogurt for garnish

Put all the ingredients except the milk, yogurt, and seasonings in a 4-quart crock pot. Fill the pot to within 2 inches from the top with water and leave to cook on a low setting overnight, or else simmer on top of the stove gently for 2 hours. Remove the meat bone and blend all the ingredients in a blender. At this stage, the soup should be very thick. Return to the pot and season with salt and pepper. Stir in the milk and warm through just before serving (do not allow to boil after adding the milk). Serve with a large dollop of yogurt and a sprig of parsley on top. Each serving (without garnish) will contain:

Calories   342   ▎   Protein   22g   ▎   Fat   2.5g   ▎   Cholesterol   7mg

VEGETABLE BEAN SOUP
12 LARGE SERVINGS

The variations on this soup are endless. You can use almost any type of bean and vegetable. This recipe was one of the most popular.

1 cup dry red kidney beans, soaked overnight

1/2 green cabbage, shredded

2-3 sliced summer squash (either zucchini or yellow crookneck)

1 eggplant, diced

1 large onion, chopped

3 carrots, shredded

2 tablespoons fresh thyme

(or 1 teaspoon dried)

2 tablespoons fresh oregano (or 1 teaspoon dried)

1/4 cup chopped fresh parsley

2 teaspoons caraway seed

2 large potatoes, cooked

To be added later:

salt and pepper to taste

juice of 2 lemons

Place all the ingredients except the salt and pepper and lemon juice in the crock pot, fill with water, and leave on a medium heat setting to cook overnight. A couple of hours before serving, add salt, pepper, and more herbs if necessary. Strain off about a pint of the liquid into a blender and blend with the potato. Return the mixture to the crock pot. Cook slowly for 1 more hour. Just before serving, stir in the lemon juice. VARIATION: Add 2 teaspoons of chopped jalapeño peppers, fresh or canned. Each serving will contain:

Calories   107   ▎   Protein   5.6g   ▎   Fat   0.5g   ▎   Cholesterol   0

Lemon Chicken Soup
SERVES 8

*1½ pounds of chicken
    with bone*

*1 tablespoon each fresh
    chopped marjoram,
    thyme, sage, and rosemary
    (or 1 teaspoon each of
    dried spices)*

2 bay leaves

½ cup rice, uncooked

2 eggs

½ cup lemon juice

1 cup milk

salt and pepper to taste

parsley to garnish

Put the chicken and herbs in a pot with 3 quarts of water. Simmer until the meat is tender and can easily be removed from the bone. Strain the liquid and return 10 cups of stock to the pot (add more water if necessary). Cook the rice in the stock until done, about 40 minutes for brown rice. Remove the chicken from the bone and cut into small pieces. Beat together the eggs and milk, then add the lemon juice and beat well. Beat 1 cup of the hot stock into the lemon-milk-egg mixture and then slowly pour the whole mixture back into the stock. Keep stirring while the mixture heats through, but do not allow to boil. Season with salt and pepper and serve hot, garnished with parsley. Each serving will contain:

Calories 162 ❙ Protein 15g ❙ Fat 6g ❙ Cholesterol 112mg

BEET AND PAPAYA SALAD
SERVES 4

If you can't get papaya, this will also work very well using diced cantaloupe.

½ pound of cooked beets, peeled and diced (or 1 can of cooked beets)

1 papaya, peeled and diced

(or 2 cups of diced large Mexican papaya)

¼ cup fresh orange juice (or 2 tablespoons lemon juice)

Mix all the ingredients in a bowl and chill in the refrigerator for at least 30 minutes before serving. Each serving will contain:

Calories 60 ▌ Protein 1g ▌ Fat 0 ▌ Cholesterol 0

BROWN RICE AND SWEET CORN SALAD
SERVES 8

1 pound brown rice, cooked

½ pound of sweet corn kernels, cooked (or 1 cup of frozen corn, or 1 can of corn, drained)

½ cup finely chopped onion

½ cup finely diced red pepper

½ cup finely diced green pepper

2 large, firm guavas, finely diced (Try kiwis or tart apples if guavas are unavailable.)

4 tablespoons vegetable oil

Heat the oil in a large wok or pan and sauté the onion until translucent. Add the diced green and red peppers and sauté until tender. Reduce the heat and stir in the corn, rice, and finally the guava. Remove from heat and season to taste. Chill in the refrigerator and stir again before serving. For a flavor accent, you may toss in a vinaigrette dressing. Each serving will contain:

Calories 372 ▌ Protein 6g ▌ Fat 16g ▌ Cholesterol 0

RED CABBAGE SALAD
SERVES 4

¹/₂ red cabbage, finely shredded
1 firm tomato, diced
¹/₂ onion, finely chopped

*1 papaya, diced
(or 2 cups diced
cantaloupe)*

Mix all the ingredients well and chill before serving. This is also delicious mixed with yogurt dill dressing. Each serving (without dressing) will contain:

Calories 63 **I** Protein 1g **I** Fat 0 **I** Cholesterol 0

YOGURT DILL DRESSING
SERVES 4

1 cup plain yogurt
*2 teaspoons crushed
dill seed*

*2 tablespoons fresh dill leaves
finely chopped (or 1
tablespoon dried dill)*
pinch of salt

Mix all the ingredients together and leave in the refrigerator for as long as possible before serving — overnight is best — to really bring out the flavor of the dill. Each serving will contain:

Calories 39 **I** Protein 3g **I** Fat 1g **I** Cholesterol 3.5mg

GARDEN SALAD

Top the following salad with your favorite vinaigrette dressing, using plenty of fresh herbs. The best thing about this salad is its bright and beckoning color!

Toss together in a bowl any combination of the following:

shredded lettuce (We used a mixture of light green-leafed lettuce and red-leafed lettuce; you can use any that is flavorful and colorful.)

thickly shredded Chinese or red cabbage

diced green and red bell peppers

finely chopped yellow and green summer squash

sliced red radishes

grated raw carrot

chopped ripe papaya or melon

finely chopped green onions or chives

BEAN & POTATO SALAD

SERVES 8

2 pounds of green beans with tips and strings removed

10-12 new white potatoes, medium size

1 cup diced onion

1/4 cup chopped chives

2 tablespoons fresh chopped basil (or 1 teaspoon dried basil)

1 teaspoon fresh thyme (or large pinch dried thyme)

2 teaspoons vegetable oil

Steam the beans and boil the potatoes until just tender but not too soft to dice. Lightly sauté the onion and chives in the oil. Dice the beans and potatoes into 1/2 inch pieces. Mix the chopped vegetables, chives, onions, oil, and fresh herbs in a large bowl and season to taste. Let stand in the refrigerator for at least an hour and toss well before serving. For a sharper flavor, toss with 2 tablespoons rice vinegar or lemon juice. Each serving will contain:

Calories 118g ❙ Protein 4g ❙ Fat 4g ❙ Cholesterol 0

CHUTNEY
SERVES 8

This recipe was brought to us by Roy Walford. It can be used as a relish or as a salad side-dish. It is best when freshly made. You can substitute honeydew melon if papaya is not available.

1/4 cup lemon juice

2 tablespoons chopped lemon rind

5 fresh figs, diced (if not available, soak dried figs overnight)

2 papayas, diced (or 4 cups diced, if using large Mexican papaya or honeydew)

1/4 cup finely diced onion

1 cup diced green pepper or green cabbage

2 medium bananas, thinly sliced

Pour the lemon juice over the figs and papaya and let the mixture sit for an hour. Then mix in the rest of the ingredients. Pack tightly into a casserole dish and cook in the microwave for 5 minutes or in a pre-heated 350-degree oven for 20 minutes. Chill before serving. Each serving will contain:

Calories 86 ▌ Protein 1g ▌ Fat 0.5g ▌ Cholesterol 0

Chapter Six

BARNYARDS & FISH PONDS

Man is the only animal that can remain on
friendly terms with the victims he intends to eat until he eats them.
Samuel Butler

Early on we decided that animals
WOULD BE AN INTEGRAL PART OF THE FARM SYSTEM. They
play the vital role of eating parts of plants grown on the farm that we cannot.
For example, after we've harvested the seed heads from the sorghum and
made it into flour, the stalks and leaves are eaten by the goats. They also love
the leaves from the peanut plants, sweet potatoes, and banana trees. The
animals' waste matter then becomes compostable material that can be returned to the soil. The animals also provide us with some fats and proteins
in the small amounts of meat, milk, and eggs we get from them, as well as
providing a welcomed variation from the otherwise vegetarian fare. The
question was, which animals to take in?

Over the years of planning and construction, we tried out different
species of each kind to select the perfect biospherian candidates. Goats were
a success from the start. We began with the full-sized Nubian goat, but we
later discovered the African pygmy goat. Its smaller size made it more
compatible with the limited food supply in the Biosphere. The smaller size

Filet of tilapia with peanut fried rice and a glass of papaya juice.

Specially bred hens and chicks in Biosphere 2.

also allows us to have more individuals, which provides a larger gene pool. Unlike the Nubian goats, pygmy goats can be bred all year long. They also give delicious milk, free of that distinctive goaty smell. As for the chickens, we knew we wanted a hardy breed that would eat a biospherian diet of greens and insects and not be dependent on commercially produced chicken feed. We went back to the jungle fowl, a very resilient bird which is probably descended from the original jungle chicken of India before they were domesticated. The birds were accustomed to foraging for themselves in the forest, so they could survive on the available diet. The jungle fowl is very territorial, so we crossed them with the 'silkie' chicken to get a calmer flock. We knew they were good egg-layers and mothers, so we hoped that we could increase the population size without the adults killing their own chicks.

The pigs turned out to be more of a problem. At first we thought we had found the perfect choice in the little Vietnamese pot-bellied pig. They are very small, have a high fat content, don't eat too much, and have a delightful disposition — the perfect biospherian. Unfortunately, the same qualities that appealed to us also appeal to pet owners across the country. The pot-bellied pig had become a very popular household pet, so when animal rights activists heard that we were planning to take them into the Biosphere as part of a farming system, they raised an outcry. We replaced the pot-bellied pig with the larger Ossabaw feral swine. Feral means 'wild,' and our boar, two sows, and their piglets proved no exception to this designation. We discovered that they would likely help themselves to a small chicken for dinner if one should accidentally wander their way. They also preferred more starch in their diet than we could afford, so after one year we were forced to take them out of the system. In the fall of 1992 we slaughtered the last two for our Thanksgiving and Christmas dinners. Maybe pigs will once again be included in future missions as part of the food and recycling system, but it seems more likely that we will experiment with other smaller animals that willingly eat a lot of green leafy matter in their diet.

We were also rather disappointed in the chickens the first year. They flatly refused to lay eggs in any significant number. Occasionally, the wretched birds would begrudgingly lay us an egg to be saved up until we had accumulated one for each of us for breakfast — a luxury which happened about once a month! Admittedly, they were last in line for the food and were fed a diet consisting mostly of vegetable peels, insects, and azolla (the high-protein water fern we grow with the rice). Even so, I could not help feeling that they were being very uncooperative and should have been more bountiful with their donations to the biospherian cause. During the second year, by saving up the residues from the threshing process which contained some grain, and feeding it to them in large quantities, we did manage to get some eggs laid and baby chicks hatched. I also thought it might help if I paid them all a little personal attention each day. I decided to give each one a name and learn to recognize them. The problem was how to find fifteen names that I could remember. Eventually I named them after my aunts, and each morning I could go down to the animal bay and greet Jessie, Phyllis, Trudy, Louise, Greta, Edith, Rusty, Hannah, and Esther, et al., by name. I'm not sure if this helped with egg laying, but at least I started to closely observe individual chicken behavior — such as who had which place in the pecking order, who would share a nesting box with whom.

The animal bay was always a delight to be in. Jane and I went down first thing every morning, milk jugs in hand. Already there would be loud bleating from the goats as soon as we walked in the door. Jane would immediately feed the goats their daily ration of roughage and high-protein fodder, while I fed the chickens and checked their egg boxes. Then came the milking. Each goat seemed to know its position in the order, but occasionally one would try to butt in out of turn. I would have to deal with the butting and pushing in the milking stall until the wrong goat was removed. I soon learned to have some yummy snacks, preferably sweet potato greens or bean hulls, to get them to stand still in the stall for milking. Their favorite game was to see how much of someone else's snack they could steal through the wires of the stall.

Unlike many people I love the smell of goats, so it was always a pleasant way for me to start the day. I could sit on my red stool squirting fresh

Jane shows off newborn kids.

SCOTT McMULLEN

Sally does the morning milking.

milk into the bucket and rest my head against the side of a warm, furry goat. Jane and I took turns with the milking, she in the evening and I in the morning and on Saturday evening. By Saturday evening there were usually lots of visitors crowding around the windows to watch. It always seemed to me that the goats were aware of this and would put on a little entertainment. The larger the group outside, the more they would lead me a dance getting in and out of the milking stall. If they could get me to chase them around the entire pen, all the better. For some reason, this never happened in the early mornings when no visitors were around.

Probably the most entertaining inhabitant of the animal bay was Buffalo Bill, our goat buck. He was also nicknamed Houdini, as he seemed to be able to get out of anything but the most tightly wired pen. If a sleepy biospherian forgot to wire the door securely, Bill would open the latch and lead the liberated goats straight for the feed bins.

This kind of incident totally infuriated Mark Nelson, who had the job of collecting much of the fodder every day. Mark often expressed his displeas-

Houdini anticipates another escape.

C. ALLAN MORGAN

ure in very entertaining, colorful language. So we decided to play a practical joke on him. One holiday weekend when we had collected two or three days' worth of fodder, we hid all the fodder in a separate storeroom. Just before Mark was to go in and dole out the evening feed, we let all the goats and pigs out of their pens. Meanwhile, Laser was hiding out of sight with his video camera. When Mark entered the pens, he was horrified at the sight of all the animals apparently 'rampaging' among the empty bins. The ensuing video footage of him chasing them all back, cursing and swearing as he went, was definitely X-rated comedy. To his credit, when he discovered it was a joke he took it all in very good humor.

Meat played a very small role in our diet. We ate it only on Sunday; usually it was no more than two or three pounds between the eight of us. As in any farming system, we had to limit the live animals to the number we could afford to feed. So at a certain age, the animals had to be slaughtered depending on the time of year and the availability of food. The slaughtering had to be a well-thought-out process since we had to make maximum use of every part of the animal. In the case of the pigs, for example, the fresh innards and blood would be brought directly to the kitchen where the heart, liver, kidneys, lungs, etc. would be cooked up in a delicious fry that night. We also made the intestines and stomach into a dish almost like pasta noodles, served with a tomato sauce. The blood was turned into sausage. I did not have a real sausage stuffer, so my first attempt at doing this left a scene in the food processing room like something out of a late-night horror movie. Eventually I improvised a sausage stuffer made with a funnel and plastic tube borrowed from Taber's analytical lab. The sausages came out very tasty. Usually all the meat cuts would be portioned out in meal-sized packages for freezing, including the head to make a posole and the trotters for soup bones. Nothing was wasted.

Another inclusion in the animal system was the tilapia fish. Fully grown these creatures can weigh about eight pounds. They are either silvery gray or pinkish white in color. The idea was that the tilapia would live in the rice paddies and eat the azolla and small water insects and provide us with an occasional fish dinner. They were known to be very hardy, able to survive in crowded conditions. Every time we harvested the rice paddies, we retrieved the fish and held them in tanks until the water in the paddies was deep enough to return them. Yet it seemed that they hardly grew. After the first year we harvested a few of the larger fish and left the rest for a second year of growth. They certainly weren't a significant part of our diet. Fish production is an area with plenty of room for development by future crews.

As I mentioned before, we had very small quantities of meat in our diet, so the variation that the animal products gave was very welcome. The milk in particular added an extra creaminess to a dessert or enabled us to make special treats such as cheese and crepes. The animals were certainly a lot of work to maintain, and sometimes we wondered if it was worth it. We will no doubt be developing this aspect of the food system more fully in time. Aside from the enhancement to our diet, their good company added a special charm to our lives. I can't imagine a morning in the Biosphere without goats to milk. ❧

STIR-FRIED PORK & VEGETABLES WITH SPICY PAPAYA SAUCE

SERVES 6

1 tablespoon oil or pork fat

2 1/2 pound pork roast (including bone)

4 medium zucchini or yellow summer squash, sliced

1/2 pound snow peas, tips and strings removed

1/2 pound carrots, thinly sliced

1 medium onion, diced

1/2 green cabbage, diced (or 1 small broccoli cut into florettes)

1 red or green pepper, diced

Roast the pork in the oven until done, about 1 1/2 to 2 hours. Pour off the drippings into a separate pan ready to make the sauce. Cut all the meat off the bone and dice it into 1-inch cubes. Now you have all the stir-fry ingredients ready to go. Next comes the sauce.

SAUCE

Dripping from the roast pork

1 teaspoon dried coriander

1 teaspoon dried ginger (or 1-inch cube fresh ginger, chopped)

1 teaspoon chili powder (or 1 fresh red chili, chopped)

1/2 medium onion, finely chopped

2 papayas (or 4 cups cubed large Mexican papaya, or honeydew or crenshaw melon)

1/4 cup brown sugar or honey (optional)

1 large cooked potato (white or sweet)

2 cups water

Heat the pork drippings in a pan and lightly sauté the spices and onion. Blend the papaya, potato, honey or sugar, and water in the blender until smooth. Add this to the pan and simmer gently for 20 minutes. Add a little more water if it is too thick.

STIR FRY

Heat the oil in a wok or frying pan. First add the onion and carrots and stir fry until tender. Then add the other vegetables and stir fry until done (crisp but not soggy). Lastly add the meat and continue to stir fry until well mixed and hot. Pour the stir-fried meat and vegetables into a serving dish and pour the hot sauce over the top. Serve immediately. Each serving will contain:

Calories 446 ❙ Protein 31g ❙ Fat 14g ❙ Cholesterol 75mg

SWEET & SOUR PORK

SERVES 8

I use pork for this recipe, but it's a great way to use up any leftover meat.

2 pounds cooked pork, diced

2 large onions, chopped

1 clove garlic, crushed

2 green peppers or 1 red and green pepper, diced

2 cups cooked beans

2 ripe bananas, sliced

1 large sweet potato, cooked

1/2 cup fresh basil (or 3 teaspoons dry basil)

2 small hot chilies

2 lemons, juiced

2 teaspoons oil

1 teaspoon salt

Blend the sweet potato, chili, basil, and lemon juice with 3 cups of water. Sauté the onion, garlic, and pepper in the oil in the bottom of a large, heavy pan or wok until tender. Add the pork and beans and stir the mixture well. Pour the potato mixture over the ingredients in the pan and bring gently to a simmer. Add the banana slices and simmer for 15 minutes. Add salt to taste. Serve with rice. Each serving will contain:

Calories 391 ❙ Protein 30g ❙ Fat 14g ❙ Cholesterol 68mg

CREAM OF CHICKEN HOT POT

SERVES 6 TO 8

2 1/2 pounds chicken with bone

2 medium onions, chopped

3 cloves garlic

2 carrots, sliced

1 pound of assorted vegetables, chopped (summer squash, cabbage, celery, turnip, rutabaga are good; avoid beets or tomatoes)

3/4 cup barley or wheat berries or 1 cup whole wheat bulgar

1 medium sweet or white potato, cooked

3 cups milk

1 tablespoon each chopped thyme, parsley, and marjoram (or 1/2 tablespoon dried)

2 bay leaves

salt and pepper to taste

Put the chicken, onion, garlic, and carrots into a crock pot with 3 quarts of water and cook overnight, or cook for about 1 hour on the stove. Lift the chicken from the broth when tender. Remove the meat from the bone and dice. Blend the broth in the blender with the potato and return it to the heat. Add the grain, chopped vegetables, and diced chicken meat. Cook until the grain is tender, about 90 minutes for wheat berries, 45 minutes for barley, 30 minutes for bulgar. Shortly before serving, stir in the milk and season to taste. Heat gently without boiling for the last ten minutes. Each serving will contain:

Calories 276 ❙ Protein 25g ❙ Fat 6g ❙ Cholesterol 73mg

Biospherian Pizza
MAKES 4 LARGE PIZZAS

The Dough

4 cups of whole-wheat flour, sifted

1 1/2 teaspoons dried yeast dissolved in 1 1/4 cups warm water

2 tablespoons vegetable oil (optional)

1 teaspoon salt

Let the yeast mixture stand until bubbly. Place the flour and salt in a bowl and mix in the oil and yeast-water mixture. Form a ball of dough, and knead for about 10 minutes adding more water if too dry or more flour if too wet. You should end up with a soft, pliable dough. Let the dough rise for 2 hours and then beat down again. Divide into four pieces and roll or press out each piece into a pizza shell, forming a slightly elevated rim around the edge to hold the filling. Put the shells on greased baking sheets.

The Topping

2 medium green peppers, chopped

2 pounds tomatoes chopped (or 2 14-ounce cans of whole stewed tomatoes)

1 large onion, finely chopped

1 medium potato, peeled and cooked

1 small stalk celery, finely chopped

1 bay leaf

1/4 cup fresh basil (or 2 teaspoons dried)

2 tablespoons fresh oregano (or 1 teaspoons dried)

2 cups of leftover chopped chicken or pork or cooked pinto beans (optional)

1 pound cream cheese, ricotta cheese, or soft goat cheese

Place all the ingredients except the potato, cheese, and meat or beans in a heavy saucepan and cover with water. Simmer gently for at least 1 hour. The longer you simmer it, the more tasty it will be. If it starts to get dry, add a little more water. After 1 hour, take some of the liquid from the pot and blend with the cooked potato. Return the blended potato to the pot and stir in well. This will help to thicken the sauce. Simmer until the sauce is thick enough to spread on the pizza shells without running. Spread the sauce on the pizzas and garnish with meat or beans if desired. Dot the top of the pizzas with cheese and bake in a 400-degree oven for 25 minutes. Each individual pizza will contain:

Calories 833 ❙ Protein 33g ❙ Fat 28g ❙ Cholesterol 62mg

TILAPIA WITH NUTS & HERBS
4 SERVINGS

4 large filets of tilapia (or any white fish)

8 ounces finely chopped nuts (We used peanuts, but almonds would also be good.)

¹/₄ cup chopped fresh basil

4 tablespoons oil

¹/₄ cup chopped fresh oregano

4 tablespoons lemon juice

Lightly steam the filets of fish until cooked. In a large non-stick pan heat the oil. Take 1/4 of the nuts and herbs and toss them in the oil. Add 1 teaspoon of lemon juice. Then take one of the filets and lightly brown it on both sides in the oil, nuts, juice, and herbs. Remove the fish from the pan and place on a serving dish. Sprinkle any herbs or nuts left in the pan over the cooked fish. Repeat for the rest of the filets. You can keep this warm in the oven, but it's best to serve as soon as possible. Each serving will contain:

Calories 612 ❙ Protein 33g ❙ Fat 49g ❙ Cholesterol 55mg

POSOLE
SERVES 8

This is a great recipe for making use of a pig's head or really tough cuts of pork, or soup bones, trotters, or any meat scraps.

3 to 4 pounds of pork meat including the bones, or one medium-sized pig's head

3 cups corn kernels

2 large onions, chopped

4 cloves garlic, finely chopped

1 cup hot green chilies, finely chopped (or less, depending on the 'heat' of the chilies)

1/2 cup oregano, chopped

1/2 cup basil, chopped

salt and pepper to taste

Place the meat in a crock pot, cover with water, and cook on a low heat overnight. If you do not have a crock pot, simmer in a heavy saucepan for at least 6 hours. Remove all the meat from the bone and return the meat to the pot. While the meat is stewing, cook the corn kernels in boiling water until tender. Add the corn to the meat pot. In a separate pan sauté the onion, chili, basil, oregano, and garlic until very well done. All these ingredients should be finely chopped. The frying will remove some of the 'heat' from the chilies, otherwise you will have a very hot posole. Mix the contents of the frying pan into the pot with the meat and corn. Simmer for at least another 6 hours. Serve in soup bowls with PICO DE GALLO.

PICO DE GALLO
This is a very spicy garnish for the POSOLE.

1/2 cup finely chopped hot chilies

1/2 cup finely chopped onions

1/4 cup finely chopped basil

1/4 cup finely chopped oregano

Mix well and sprinkle over the POSOLE. Each serving will contain:

Calories 398 ▮ Protein 42g ▮ Fat 18g ▮ Cholesterol 119mg

FISH PIE

SERVES 6

10-inch pie dish, lined with a well-salted pie crust

2 large potatoes, peeled and cooked

1 pound of tilapia (or any white fish)

1/4 cup chopped parsley

1/4 cup milk

1 tablespoon dry tarragon

2 lemons, juiced

2 eggs, lightly beaten

slices of lemon and parsley sprigs for garnish

salt and pepper to taste

Lightly steam the fish until cooked, remove any bones, and break into small flakes. Mash the potatoes (do not purée). Fold the fish and other ingredients into the mashed potato. Season the mixture with salt and pepper to taste and pour the mixture into the pie shell. Bake at 350 degrees for about 30 minutes. Cut the pie into generous slices and serve with a parsley and lemon garnish. Each serving will contain:

Calories 431 ❙ Protein 27g ❙ Fat 10g ❙ Cholesterol 134mg

HOT FISH SAUCE

SERVES 8

This dish should be served on a bed of brown rice or poured over mashed sweet or white potatoes.

2 pounds tilapia (or any white fish)

1/2 cup finely chopped hot green chilies (or 1/4 cup canned, chopped jalapeños)

1 cup finely chopped onion

3 pounds tomatoes or 1 28-ounce can of tomatoes

2 finely chopped garlic cloves

1/2 cup fresh basil (or 3 tablespoons dried basil)

1/2 cup fresh oregano (or 3 tablespoons dried oregano)

2 tablespoons cooking oil

salt and pepper to taste

Heat the oil in a pan and sauté the onion, chilies, and garlic until well done. Blend the tomatoes and herbs in the blender and add to the frying pan. Lightly steam the fish and remove the flesh from the bone. Break the flesh into small flakes and add to the pan. Gently simmer the mixture in the pan for about 1 hour. The mixture should be thick but pourable. If necessary, add a little water. Season to taste. Each serving will contain:

Calories 285 ▌ Protein 3g ▌ Fat 16g ▌ Cholesterol 62mg

Chapter Seven

A Moveable Feast

To eat is human — to stuff is divine.
Marshall Efron

After graduating from school, I spent several years as a volunteer organizer of an agricultural extension project in northern Bihar, India. Bihar is a region well known for its droughts, famines, and desertification. Providing an adequate amount of food to keep life and limb together is the major concern of most of the inhabitants. The people I lived and worked with were hill people. They combined a slash-and-burn agricultural system with hunting and gathering in the surrounding jungle. They were not Hindus but believed in the powers of natural spirits which lived in trees, other jungle plants, and crops.

Of major importance in their lives were feast days, held in honor of the first harvest of every new crop. They were celebrated by drinking great quantities of home-made beer brewed from date palm sap and eating a large amount of the crop just harvested. There were also feasts for weddings, funerals, and to celebrate the birth of sons. In fact, there were times when feasts came thick and fast, and whole villages would be drunk for days at a

Banana cheesecake with a glass of banana wine.

The kitchen bursts with cooks preparing for a feast.

ABIGAIL ALLING

time. Hangover victims frequently appeared at the door of my hut, pleading for cures for their headaches and sour stomachs from my small medical clinic.

I never fully understood the importance of feasts to these people until many years later while living in Biosphere 2. For the first time in my life, the availability of food was restricted and the edge of hunger was an almost constant companion. We eagerly anticipated the days on which we could stuff our bellies full and then sit back and enjoy the sensations of satisfaction. Over the first few months, feasting became firmly established as one of the most important features of our lives, just as it was in Bihar.

The feasts developed in magnitude and magnificence over time. Our first one was on Thanksgiving in November 1991 and set the style for many to come. That morning the kitchen was bursting with cooks. My main job was to keep them all well supplied with whatever they needed. Taber roasted a rack of pork ribs to perfection. Laser and Gaie made our first sweet potato pie (sweetened with banana), a dish which was to become a great favorite. I experimented with the first cheesecake I ever made without sugar or eggs. It was then that I realized that I could take all my favorite recipes and use substitutes for the ingredients that weren't available, providing I kept to the same type of ingredient (wet, dry, sweet, etc.). They would usually turn out.

At lunch time we gathered in our second-story lounge and opened the doors to the balcony that overlooks the IAB. We set out all the food on one table in a colorful arrangement and just stood admiring it for some time before digging in. The ribs, sweet potato pie, and cheesecake were joined by a beautiful garden salad, chutney, fried rice, gravy, and a plate of stir-fried vegetables. We spent that afternoon happily chewing and talking.

As the months passed, everyone developed individual specialties. Taber learned how to make pig's head *posole*, a dish indigenous to his native New Mexico. Roy developed a delicious chutney made from papayas and figs. My cheesecakes improved. Jane perfected her tomato soup, and Laser and Gaie went on to make ever more delicious sweet potato pies. Laser was also

The balcony was the scene of many festivities.

the crepe master in the Biosphere. One evening he made a beautiful-looking plate of crepes garnished with fresh fruit and put them into the oven to warm. When he came back to remove them, to his horror the oven (a very fancy, German, electric one with a large array of features that no one had really bothered to investigate) had locked itself and gone into a self-cleaning cycle. He ran into the dining room to tell us all of the problem. Imagine eight biospherians all diving for the operating manual at once and thumbing through it desperately to bring the oven back under human control! Eventually someone thought of turning the whole thing off at the breaker. The crepes were saved!

Lacking outside entertainments, our birthdays became very special. And since they are spaced fairly regularly throughout the year, we always had one to look forward to. For variety we chose different locations for the meals and decorated each according to a theme.

The first really memorable one was the beach party we held for Jane. It was in late autumn, so it was already dark when I carried all the dishes down to the beach. This was not an easy maneuver since the route from the kitchen to the beach is an obstacle course of heavy doors and stairs through the dimly lit basement. Once at the beach, we arranged the food on a cloth- covered table top under a birthday chandelier made from a camera tripod decorated with Christmas tree lights. Since we can't have open flames in the Biosphere, no candles allowed! It really was a bizarre scene as we sat on the sand listening to the waves and toasting Jane's health with homemade banana wine.

Mark Nelson's birthday dinner was in our re-creation of an Indian bazaar, where we all reclined on heaps of cushions surrounded by silk hangings backlit with colored lights, the air filled with sitar music. For Laser's birthday we turned the library into a discotheque, with dazzling sound and lights. My thirty-seventh birthday was celebrated with a black-tie dinner held in our exercise room, transformed for the occasion by the addition of a magnificent dining table, a chandelier made with gold paper, and beautiful flower arrangements. All eight guests dressed in their very best, the gentlemen in suits and ties and the ladies in evening gowns. It had been so long since I had seen the crew dressed like this, that it was like looking at seven completely different people! Admittedly the attire looked a little baggy, as everything had been bought to fit our weights before closure. It was a very elegant evening. In contrast to mine, Roy's birthday was a *lungi* party. A lungi is a type of garment worn by men in India which is basically a piece of cloth wrapped around the waist that hangs down to the ankles. It can be worn like a sarong by women. We all came wrapped in colorful cloths and sprawled around in the lounge overlooking the agriculture area.

The feasts developed in magnitude and magnificence over time.

ABIGAIL ALLING

Each feast seemed to become more elaborate than the last. I began thinking well in advance about what goodies I would need to have in store for the next one. Many days before a birthday we would start saving all the ripe fruit, especially the figs, to decorate the cake. These birthday cakes were probably one of the greatest challenges, since we had no butter and usually no eggs. Eventually I hit on an adaptation of banana bread for the cake base and then elaborately decorated the base with fruit sauces and fresh fruit to make up for the lack of frosting. I think this was when I felt our limitation of flavors the most. Our cocoa trees in the rainforest were healthy but small, and clearly would not be producing cocoa pods for several years. The coffee trees only produced enough for a very occasional cup of coffee, certainly not enough to flavor a cake with. We brought vanilla orchids in with us, but they did not produce fruits during the first mission. Some of these luxurious items will probably be more plentiful for future crews. We're the ones who had to improvise!

Pizza became the traditional birthday entree in the Biosphere. The toppings varied greatly according to the cook, but all had a layer of goat cheese and were accompanied by a large salad and a bottle of wine. My first attempt at wine-making produced six bottles of good banana wine. After that I had several failures and produced some very fine vinegar. I occasionally made rice wine using a special yeast from Nepal where it's used to make a traditional drink called *chung*. My chung was potent but very sour; one had to be determined to imbibe in order to drink it. I came to realize that wine was a very important part of the feasting. It helped everyone to relax and get into the spirit of party time and festivity, so I continued to experiment with different brews. My main problem was finding the raw ingredients. Anything with enough starch or sugar in it to make alcohol could rarely be spared for drinking.

I very much doubt if I will ever again savor a festive meal as much as those we enjoyed in Biosphere 2. Every mouthful was appreciated, the color and aroma of every dish was noticed and commented on. Of course, our keen appetites enhanced the flavors, but the fact that all the food was freshly grown by our own hands made a big difference.

The highlight of the feasts were the desserts, so we would make several favorites. The recipes below are, on the whole, low in calories compared with most desserts and use the natural flavors of fruits for sweetener. For more sweetness, sugar or honey can be added to most of them. ❧

SWEET POTATO PIE
SERVES 8

This was the first pie baked inside Biosphere 2. Laser and Gaie created it, and we ate it for our first Thanksgiving dinner after the sweet potato harvest. It immediately became our all-time favorite. You can use any pie crust recipe you like including the 'pat-in' variety. I have included the pie crust recipe the biospherians used especially for those who are watching calories or cholesterol intake, because it contains no fat. This recipe makes one 10-inch pie.

PIE CRUST

1 1/4 *cups of whole-wheat flour*
pinch of salt

1 cup of puréed banana
(2 medium bananas)

Mix the flour and salt and work into a soft dough with the puréed banana. If the dough is too stiff, add a little milk. The dough can either be rolled out with a rolling pin or patted into place in a lightly greased, 10-inch pie pan or quiche dish. Bake the crust for 10 minutes in a preheated 350-degree oven before adding the filling.

FILLING

2 cups cooked, mashed, sweet potatoes
(2 large potatoes)

1 1/4 *cups mashed banana*
(2 large or 3 small bananas)

1/2 *cup of plain low-fat yogurt*

1 large egg (optional)
1 teaspoon cinnamon
1 teaspoon dry ginger (or 1/2-*inch cube of fresh ginger, mashed)*
pinch of nutmeg
pinch of ground cloves

Serving the sweet tooth in Biosphere 2.

Blend all of the ingredients together in a blender until very smooth and creamy. Pour the filling in the pre-baked pie crust and bake for 30 minutes at 350 degrees. Allow to cool for at least 20 minutes before serving so that the filling sets well. In general, when cooking with bananas, I find that the fillings bake to a firm set much more quickly than with a traditional egg & milk custard filling, so be careful not to overbake. If a sweeter filling is desired, add 1/4 cup of honey and blend with the rest of the ingredients. Best served while still a little warm with a dollop of yogurt on top of each slice. VARIATION: This can also be made with pumpkin. Each serving will contain:

Calories 216 ❙ Fat 2g ❙ Protein per serving 6g ❙ Cholesterol per serving 35mg

BANANA CHEESECAKE
SERVES 8

I invented this recipe for our first December Solstice feast. This marked the shortest day of the year, and from then on the days would only get longer with more hours of sunshine to pour down on our crops; something to really celebrate in the Biosphere! Compared with other cheesecakes it is very low-calorie. The eggs are optional; it will set perfectly well without any. I used cream cheese made from our goat's milk but you can use any soft white cream cheese, including the low-fat kind. Preheat oven to 350 degrees.

1 10-inch pie crust, pre-baked for 10 minutes (see sweet potato pie recipe)

12 ounces cream cheese

1 1/2 cups plain yogurt

2 cups puréed bananas (4 medium bananas)

Optional:

2 eggs

1/4 cup honey

Blend all the ingredients in the blender until smooth and creamy. Pour into the pre-baked pie crust and bake for 30 minutes or until set. Allow to cool before serving. You can top with a layer of yogurt and decorate with any fresh fruit (try a mixture of strawberry and banana slices). Serve well chilled. Without the eggs and honey each serving will contain:

Calories 410 ❙ Protein 11g ❙ Fat 18g ❙ Cholesterol 49mg

BIOSPHERIAN RICE PUDDING
SERVES 8

We always used bananas as the main sweetener for this fruity version of rice pudding. However, you may use any puréed fruit as the flavoring. If you want a sweeter taste add a few spoonfuls of honey.

3 cups of brown rice

2 cups low-fat milk

2 cups water (or more)

4 large, or 6 small bananas, puréed

1 cup or more of chopped fresh fruits (We used a combination of banana, fig, guava, and strawberry, but you can use any fruit.)

Optional: 1/4 cup honey

Variation: Try chopped dried fruit such as apricots or apples instead of, or along with, the fresh fruit.

Wash the rice and place it in a double boiler. Pour in the milk and just enough water until the fluid is approximately 2 inches above the level of the rice. Cook over the double boiler for about 1 1/2 hours or until the rice is soft. Keep checking to make sure there is liquid in the pot, and be prepared to add up to another cup of water, a little at a time, to keep the mixture moist. When the rice is cooked, stir in the pureed bananas, and add honey if desired. Stir in the chopped fruit. Pour the mixture into a deep baking dish and bake in a 350-degree oven for 20 minutes. Serve hot, topped with a dollop of yogurt. Try this for a hearty breakfast dish instead of the usual bowl of cereal. You can always make it the night before and warm it in the microwave for breakfast. Each serving will contain:

Calories 377 ❙ Protein 8 g ❙ Fat 3g ❙ Cholesterol 4.5mg

FRUIT SMOOTHIES
SERVES 8

*2 pounds of fresh fruit
(Bananas, papayas, apples,
guavas, strawberries, figs,
and kumquats were used in
the Biosphere, but you can use
just about any combination of
fruit you like.)*

3 cups of plain yogurt

*1 teaspoon of finely chopped
mint leaves*

Whip all the ingredients in the blender and pour into individual glasses. You can either refrigerate and serve as a creamy drink or you can freeze it for about an hour (use plastic glasses for this) and serve as a frozen dessert. The variations are endless. This makes a delicious low calorie snack.

Note for parents: poured into plastic popsicle forms and frozen, this is an ideal treat for children.

Nutritional content will vary according to the fruit you use. These figures are for 1 pound of banana and 1 pound of papaya mixed (one of our most popular combinations). Each serving will contain:

Calories 157 ▎ Protein 6g ▎ Fat 2g ▎ Cholesterol 5mg

SPICY FRUIT ROLL
12 SLICES

Because tropical fruits were abundant in the Biosphere, I always used a mixture of banana, fig, and papaya, but you can use almost any fruit to fill this roll. With firmer fruits like apples or pears, you may want to pre-cook them to soften them first.

1 tablespoon yeast

1 teaspoon salt

3 tablespoons honey (optional)

2-3 tablespoons dried spices

(use your favorites: cinnamon, ginger, cloves, allspice)

6 $^1/_2$ cups flour (whole-wheat or unbleached white)

1 pound or more of soft fruit

Dissolve the yeast, honey, and salt in 3 cups of lukewarm water. Stir in 3 cups of flour and mix well. Let the mixture rise for 15 minutes. Stir in the spices and add the other 3 1/2 cups of flour. Form the dough into a ball and knead for 10 minutes. If the dough is sticky, work in some more flour as you knead. Form the kneaded dough into a long roll about 1-foot long and then roll it out to a rectangle approximately 8 x 12 inches. If you like your pastry sweet, at this stage you may want to sprinkle on a thin layer of sugar or spread on a thin layer of honey. Slice the fruit thinly and arrange it in a layer over the dough. Roll the dough up like a jelly roll and cut it into 1-inch slices. Lay the slices on a greased baking sheet and leave them for 15 minutes to rise again. Bake in a 350-degree oven for 45 minutes. Once the rolls are cool, they can be glazed with honey and chopped nuts, but they are also very good plain if you're counting calories. Each slice will contain:

Calories 252 ▮ Protein 9g ▮ Fat 1g ▮ Cholesterol 0

QUICK BANANA ICE CREAM
8 LARGE SERVINGS

3 pounds bananas   *6 cups milk*

Blend the banana and milk together in the blender. Pour the mixture into a freezer container and place in the freezer. After one hour mash up the mixture with a spoon so that it does not set into a solid lump, and put it back into the freezer for another hour or until you want to serve it. Top with chopped fresh fruit or your favorite ice cream toppings. Gobble this up quickly, because it will begin to melt almost immediately. This is a light, refreshing version of ice cream and is very quick to make. Each serving will contain:

Calories 236 ▮ Protein 8g ▮ Fat 4g ▮ Cholesterol 13mg

FRUIT SQUARES
12 LARGE SQUARES

You can use almost any fruit to fill these squares. If you use berries, make sure they are well drained. If you use hard fruit such as apples or pears, pre-cook them until you can lightly mash them. I usually used banana or fig for the filling and papaya to make the jam topping.

DOUGH

1 tablespoon yeast

4 tablespoons honey (optional)

5 cups flour (whole-wheat or unbleached white)

1 1/2 teaspoons salt

4 teaspoons grated orange or lemon rind

1 teaspoon fennel seed

1 teaspoon anise seed

Fruit filling suggestions:

mashed banana

mashed figs

any combination of dried fruits, stewed and drained

mashed, pre-cooked apples or pears

well-drained berries

Dissolve the yeast and honey in 1 1/2 cups of lukewarm water and leave for 10 minutes. Put the rest of the dough ingredients into a bowl and add the yeast mixture. Work the dough into a ball and knead for 10 minutes. Let rise for one hour. Lightly grease an 8 x 12-inch baking pan. Divide the dough in half, and roll out the first half into an oblong shape and press it into the bottom of the baking pan. Spread on the fruit layer and then roll out the other half of the dough, and put this on top. You may have to do a little patching with pieces of dough, but it is very pliable and you can press it into place with your fingers. Let rise for 15 minutes, then bake in a 350-degree oven for 45 minutes or until golden brown on top. Cut into squares as soon as you take it out of the oven and leave them to cool on a baking rack. As soon as they are cool, spread with a thin layer of fruit jam or chopped nuts and honey. Each square will contain:

Calories 207 ▌ Protein ▌ 7g ▌ Fat 1g ▌ Cholesterol 0

FRUIT CUSTARD PIE
SERVES 8
ONE 10-INCH PIE

This is a variation of the UPSIDE DOWN FRUIT CUSTARD (page 94) baked in a pie shell. The banana custard flavor goes very well with any berries, figs, papaya, or even slices of banana.

1 10-inch pie crust, pre-baked for 10 minutes

2 cups soft fresh fruit or canned fruit

1 white potato, cooked

4 bananas

1 1/2 cups yogurt

2 eggs (optional)

Blend the banana, potato, yogurt, and egg in a blender until the mixture is really smooth and creamy. Pour into the pie shell. Arrange the fruit decoratively on the custard and bake in a 350-degree oven for 30 minutes or until the mixture is firmly set. Each serving will contain:

Calories 223 ❙ Protein 8g ❙ Fat 3g ❙ Cholesterol 71g

CREAM CHEESE

Makes approximately 1 pound of cheese. This will vary according to the fat content of the milk used.

8 cups of whole milk
1 teaspoon of freeze-dried
  yogurt culture
(available at health
food stores)
a piece of cheese cloth

Scald the milk, put it into a jug and leave it to stand until it is warm to touch. Add the yogurt culture and let it stand covered at room temperature for 24 hours. By this time the milk should have curdled, and you should have thick white cheese curds floating in a watery yellow liquid. If not, warm the mixture slightly, add two tablespoons of lemon juice, and leave it at room temperature again until curdled. Strain the mixture through a cheese cloth. To do this you can tie up the curds into a ball in the cheese cloth and tie the ends of the cheese cloth to the jug handle leaving the ball to drip inside the jug. Put the whole jug in the refrigerator and let it drain for 24 hours. When you untie the cheese cloth you will have a ball of delicious cream cheese. This is good as is, or you can add a variety of flavorings such as a pinch of salt and some chopped herbs, or minced garlic, chopped chives, or finely minced onion. This cheese will freeze very well if you don't want to use it right away. The liquid that drains into the jug can be used in soups and stews.

CREAM CHEESE FROSTING

I first made this frosting to celebrate the anniversary of our first year inside Biosphere 2. We had decided to have a cake-cutting ceremony, with the biospherians having their cake inside and all the anniversary friends and visitors having their cake on the outside at the same time. I knew the outside cake would be frosted, and I wanted ours to look just as appealing. I made the cake using the banana bread recipe, adding just a little more banana to make the mixture a little heavier. I covered the cake with the cream cheese frosting and decorated it with fresh fruit. It looked magnificent and I am sure I saw a few envious faces peering through the glass as we cut the cake into eight huge slices and tucked in.

1/2 cup orange or lemon juice
8 ounces cream cheese
2 tablespoons honey (optional)

1/2 teaspoon grated orange or lemon zest

Blend all the ingredients in a blender, then chill until thick and spreadable. Divided into eight portions, each portion will contain:

Calories 116 ❙ Protein 2g ❙ Fat 10g ❙ Cholesterol 31mg

UPSIDE DOWN FRUIT CUSTARD
SERVES 8

You can either use 8 individual creme caramel molds to make this desert or you can use two ordinary pie dishes and serve it in slices.

Approximately 2 pounds of any fresh, soft fruit for the topping (banana, fig, melon, papaya, apple, apricot, peach)

8 bananas *(You can replace up to $^1/4$ of this with honey if you want a sweeter dessert.)*

2 *medium sweet potatoes, cooked*

3 *cups milk or yogurt*

Slice the fruit and arrange decoratively in the bottom of the molds or the pie pans. If you use pie pans, oil them lightly first. Blend the banana, potato, and milk in a blender until the mixture is really smooth and creamy. Pour the mixture over the fruit and bake in a 350-degree oven for 30 minutes or until the mixture is firmly set (test with a knife inserted into the center of the custard). Remove from the oven and allow to cool, then place in the refrigerator for at least an hour. Turn out the custards onto a serving plate so the fruit shows on top. A dollop of yogurt makes a nice final touch. Each serving will contain:

Calories 321 ▮ Protein 6g ▮ Fat 3g ▮ Cholesterol 7mg

BANANA BREAD PUDDING

TWO 10-INCH ROUND LAYERS

1 tablespoon yeast

1 cup warm water

4 cups whole-wheat flour

6 large bananas, puréed in the blender

2 tablespoons grated orange or lemon zest

¹/₂ cup chopped dried fruit or raisins

Preheat the oven to 350 degrees. Put the tablespoon of yeast in the warm water, stir well, and leave for five minutes until it starts foaming. Put the pureed banana in a bowl and add the yeast mixture to it. Let stand for about 15 minutes. Stir in the flour, lemon or orange zest, and the chopped fruit or raisins. Place the mixture in two 10-inch round lightly oiled cake pans and leave to rise for 15 minutes. Bake for 40 to 50 minutes until done. Test by inserting a knife in the center of the bread. If it comes out clean, the bread is done. This bread has a very dense, pudding-like consistency. The layers can be frosted with CREAM CHEESE FROSTING. Divided into eight portions, each portion will contain:

Calories 340 ▮ Fat 2g ▮ Protein 10g ▮ Cholesterol 0

CREPES
TWENTY-FOUR 8-INCH CREPES

3 cups whole-wheat flour   *3 eggs*
1 teaspoon salt   *4 cups milk*

Mix the dry ingredients. Separate the egg yolks from the whites. Beat the egg yolks into the milk and work the liquid into the dry mixture until smooth. Beat the egg whites until stiff and fold into the mixture. Lightly oil a non-stick pan and heat it over a high flame. Drop the mixture into the pan, a ladle full at a time. Cook on one side until the crepe just comes away from the pan then flip it over and cook the other side. Turn out the crepe onto a plate and spoon a column of filling towards one end. Roll up the crepe and serve immediately or keep them warm in a low oven until all are made.

FILLING

We used lightly stewed soft fruits for the filling or a mixture of cream cheese and fruit. Try this:

Take 1 pound of soft cream cheese or ricotta cheese. Finely chop up any soft fruit (apple, banana, papaya, fig, melon, strawberries) and mix into the cheese with a squeeze of lemon juice and a little honey. Using 4 large bananas for the filling, each crepe will contain:

Calories 163 ❙ Protein 6g ❙ Fat 8g ❙ Cholesterol 58mg

BIOSPHERIAN BAKED DOUGHNUTS
MAKES 16 DOUGHNUTS

1 medium potato

1 cup milk

4 medium bananas, puréed

4 teaspoons dried yeast

5 cups whole-wheat flour

Cook the potato and save 4 tablespoons of the cooking water. Allow the reserved cooking water to cool to room temperature. Mix the dried yeast with the warm potato water and let stand until foamy. Scald the milk and allow to cool to lukewarm, then mix in the banana puree. Add the yeast to the milk and banana mixture. Mash the potato with a potato masher and add it to the mixture. Slowly work in the flour. Let the mixture rise for 1 hour, then knead on a floured surface for 5 to 8 minutes. Roll out with a rolling pin to 1/2 inch thick and cut into doughnuts with a doughnut cutter. (If you don't have one, improvise. I used a glass jar to cut the outside and a pill bottle to cut the inside hole.) Place on a baking tray and let rise again for 40 minutes. Bake in the oven at 425 degrees for about 12 minutes or until brown on top. Put the topping on immediately and leave to cool on a rack.

TOPPINGS

In the Biosphere we used fruit jams for the topping but there are many varieties you could try: glazed icings, honey and chopped nuts, or brush with melted butter and coat with confectioners sugar. Each doughnut without a topping will contain:

Calories 170 **|** Protein 6g **|** Fat 1g **|** Cholesterol 1mg

MINT & LEMON GRASS TEA

¹/₂ cup of fresh mint leaves

2 or 3 blades of lemon grass

Put the mint and lemon grasss in the bottom of the tea pot and pour in the boiling water. Leave to steep for at least 10 minutes. Serve hot or iced.

TROPICAL JUICE
MAKES EIGHT 1-CUP SERVINGS

3 pounds of papaya, skinned
  or 3 pounds of cantaloupe

2 large bananas, very ripe

up to 8 cups water

4 teaspoons lemon juice

1 teaspoon dry ginger or
  1/2-inch cube of fresh ginger,
  finely ground

Blend all the ingredients in the blender and serve chilled. If you prefer it sweeter add sugar or honey to taste. Each cup will contain:

Calories 98 ▌ Protein 1g ▌ Fat 0.25g ▌ Cholesterol 0

BANANA WINE
ABOUT 3 BOTTLES

1 1/2 pounds dried banana

1 gallon hot water

1/2 teaspoon yeast nutrient*

1 sachet wine yeast*

Campden tablets (optional)*

fermentation jar
(with an air-lock)*

*These specialty ingredients can be purchased in a hobby shop that sells brewing and wine-making supplies. It is important that all utensils used for wine-making be sterile to avoid contamination. The Campden tablets are dissolved in water and used as a disinfectant, but you can use bleach or boiling.

Chop the dried banana and stir into the gallon of hot water along with the yeast nutrient. When the mixture has cooled to 70 degrees, add the yeast. Cover the container with a plastic sheet and leave to ferment for seven days stirring daily. Strain out the solids through a cheese cloth or sieve and place the liquid in a one-gallon fermentation jar with an air lock. After three months, and again after six months, siphon off the clear liquid leaving the sediment behind. As soon as the wine is clear and stable (about 10 months), you can bottle it.

Chapter Eight

SEASONAL CYCLES

Experience is not what happens to a man;
it is what man does with what happens to him.
Aldous Huxley

BY THE SECOND YEAR OF THE EXPERIMENT
WE HAD ALL, TO SOME EXTENT, ADAPTED TO THE CYCLES
OF THE BIOSPHERE AND OUR NEW LIFE STYLE. Rice harvests,
wheat harvests, the first flowering of the hyacinth beans in the fall, picking
the first good tomato harvest in the spring, or the first early snow peas became
seasonal landmarks.

Although our variations in climate were far less dramatic than the
variations outside, we also felt the effects of the onset of winter. Shorter day
lengths meant less time to work in the early morning, my favorite time for
farming. Colder days outside meant more condensation on the glass, and
thick sweaters for the evenings. I often watched our visitors on the outside
during winter struggling against pouring rain and high winds to see the
Biosphere, waving in at me from under their plastic rain macs and giving me
a thumbs-up sign. I was filled with admiration for them and touched by the
knowledge that people were so interested and determined to see the project.

A quiet evening in the Biosphere 2 library.

Farm work averaged about 3 hours a day per person.

I was sure that they must envy me 'tucked-up' in my cozy tropical Biosphere. The time passed unbelievably quickly. When we planted the first of the winter wheat or harvested the autumn's rice crop, I was always thinking to myself, "Is it really a year ago that we last did this? It seems like just last week!"

By the fall of 1992, I had formed a routine for the food management which became an integral part of my life. The chores formed a comfortable pattern that kept all the hard work and the little crises of farming in a realistic perspective. Every Wednesday I spent the morning grinding the flour for the week, weighing out the week's dried food, and moving it from the store room to the kitchen. When there was plenty of milk, I saved a little each day and on Saturday made a batch of delicious goat cheese. Every other day I made enough sourdough bread dough for two days and then gave it to the cooks to make into fresh loaves of bread or buns for breakfast. And, of course, our birthdays came and went regularly to punctuate my routine with the huge cakes and great feasting.

The memory of what it took to produce an adequate diet for eight people from one half acre of land is something I will always keep with me. Overall it took at least one third of our working day, and for some of us a lot longer. After a while I became expert at knowing how many 'man-hours' it would take to do a certain job. For example, replanting a wheatfield after the soil had been prepared would take four people one and a half hours. Threshing the wheat from one of the larger plots would take five man-hours. This knowledge became very important in planning our crews, but of course could only be learned through repeated experience.

Taber tending the crops.

MARK NELSON

My attitude towards food and what constitutes a good, healthy diet has certainly changed for the better, as has the shape of my body, now some twenty-five pounds lighter. But more than the weight loss and the lower cholesterol, the satisfaction of producing everything we ate with our own hands was the unique experience for all of us. It would be almost impossible to repeat it out in the wider world in this age of easy-to-use stores, mass distribution, and the highly mechanized agri-business of the late twentieth century.

One thing we have realized for certain: we were only at the beginning of developing this type of system. The most exciting thing now is to look at how to improve and build on what we have learned, how to increase our yields along with diversity of foods. Pest control, utilization of sunlight, pollination,

A sunflower brightens our garden.

GILL C. KENNY

and maturation are all important aspects to be studied on an on-going basis. There are many foods I would like to see studied and tested for future possibilities, such as the yams and other starchy root crops that are used widely in the tropics and the ever-increasing number of newly developed grains and legumes.

In this book, I have offered you some of the basic, hearty recipes that we all enjoyed, while describing how and why we used these particular ingredients. Some of these foods are rarely prepared in the home these days, but learning to do this on a regular basis has been a tremendously rewarding experience for me. I hope others will try some of these dishes along with the more familiar fare. As for the luxury dishes we all love to indulge in at least once in a while, maybe a future biospherian cookbook will include more of those or even foods that we have not even thought of yet.

Bon appetit — eat well and wisely!

ABOUT THE AUTHOR

After graduating from high school in London, England, Sally Silverstone traveled widely, including a year spent in East Africa. She then returned to England to complete a degree in Applied Social Studies at Sheffield Hallam University. Her fascination with traditional cultures in remote areas took her to India and later to Puerto Rico where she spent several years working on food and agricultural projects with native populations. For the last nine years Sally Silverstone has worked with the Biosphere 2 team, serving as manager of the design studio and the coordinator of the Biospherian Training Program. In 1991 she entered Biosphere 2 as co-captain and food systems manager of the first crew to inhabit this unique research project.

INDEX